THE FRENCH CIVIL CODE

University of Texas at Austin Studies in Foreign and Transnational Law

General Editors: Professor Sir Basil Markesinis and Dr Jörg Fedtke

Other titles in this series include:

Judicial Recourse to Foreign Law: A New Source of Inspiration?
Sir B Markesinis & J Fedtke

Italian Private law
G Alpa & V Zenovich

International Negotiation in the 21st Century
A Plantcy

The Protection of Human Rights in German and English Law
J Fedtke & C O'Cinneide

Spanish Private Law
M Martin-Casals

THE FRENCH CIVIL CODE

Jean-Louis Halpérin
Professor of Law at
l'Ecole Normale
supérieure (Paris)

Translated by
Tony Weir
Fellow of Trinity College,
Cambridge

Routledge
Taylor & Francis Group
LONDON AND NEW YORK

First published in French as Le Code civil

First published in English 2006 as *The French Civil Code*
by Routledge

The name of University College London (UCL) is a registered trade mark
used by Routledge with the consent of the owner

Routledge is an imprint of the Taylor & Francis Group, an informa business

Taylor & Francis
2 Park Square, Milton Park, Abingdon, Oxon, OX14 4RN, UK

Published in the USA
by Routledge
711 Third Avenue, New York, NY 10017

Typeset in Sabon by Newgen Imaging Systems, Chennai, India

British Library Cataloguing in Publication Data
A catalogue record for this book is available from the British Library

Library of Congress Cataloging in Publication Data
A catalog record for this book has been requested

ISBN 10: 1-84472-131-0 (pbk)
ISBN 10: 1-84472-132-9 (hbk)

ISBN 13: 978-1-84472-131-3 (pbk)
ISBN 13: 978-1-84472-132-0 (hbk)

Contents

Foreword

The *University of Texas at Austin Studies in Foreign and Transnational Law* has, as the title of the series suggests, a double purpose.

The first is to help publish books treating various subjects of foreign law in the hope that they will satisfy the growing need of universities as well as practitioners to learn more about foreign legal systems (and we shall interpret foreign to include not just private or public law but, in appropriate circumstances, all types of transnational law as well). This wide definition is meant to underline our belief that the world is shrinking and that there is, therefore, a growing need to expand our knowledge about other legal orders, national or supranational. This trend will keep growing in the future; with national boarders becoming porous, the travel of ideas can no longer be stopped at national frontiers. At the same time, we intend to publish books telling us how to study and compare legal systems and not just describing them. So we here use comparative law in the way that German jurists do, that is by placing the emphasis on the comparative *method (Rechtsvergleichung)* and not *law (droit comparé)*.

Our second aim, as the title of our series again suggests, is to provide a new example, possibly the first, of a transatlantic academic *publishing* venture. For though student exchange programmes between English and oversees universities have increased over the years, academic co-operation has, in law, on the whole remained modest in scale when it comes to other forms of legal co-operation (for instance, professorial and judicial exchanges). The first of the editors of this series has thus spent his entire professional life creating such exchanges, mainly between English (Cambridge, Queen Mary and Westfield College, Oxford, and University College London), Dutch (Leiden and Utrecht), French (Paris I and II, *Cour de cassation* and soon, we hope, the *Ecole Normale Supérieure*), German (Bonn, Cologne, Munich), Italian (Genoa, Siena, Rome) and American (Cornell, Michigan, University of Texas at Austin) institutions. The present series thus represents a further extension of this co-operation, taking it into the publishing field; and it is based on the University of Texas at Austin and University College London link which he helped forge ten years ago and which will soon enter an even more ambitious stage in its life.

The first volume of the series appropriately starts with an excellent small monograph about the French Civil Code, one of the world's most famous codifications. Though this has not escaped the ravages of time, as the text of this book recounts, it has also revealed some of the greatest strengths of the two geniuses who can claim paternity to it: Napoleon and Portalis.

To praise so openly Napoleon, especially when it has – alas – become fashionable in Anglo-American circles to indulge in 'French bashing', may appear odd; but the elegant last appendix, reproducing the calm judgment of an eminent historian (not known, incidentally, for being a friend of Napoleon's) should help remind all but the most closed-minded of how important this document has proved to be, especially from a sociological and constitutional point of view.

Portalis, the main, but not sole, technical genius behind the text is also little known in this country except by the few who interest themselves in such matters. But writing in 1797, while in self-imposed exile in northern Germany, he made, among others, the following beautiful remark which we dare not render into English lest we destroy the harmony between thought and stylistic elegance:

> « Il existe entre la simple érudition et la véritable science la différence que l'on remarque entre le jugement et la mémoire. La simple érudition n'est qu'un dépôt de faits et de matériaux divers; la science suppose un dépôt mais elle le transforme en propriété et elle en règle l'usage. On est érudit par la multitude ou la masse des choses acquises; on est savant par la manière de les choisir et de les employer. L'homme purement érudit possède; le vrai savant jouit. La science aide le génie; presque toujours la simple érudition le tue. »

These words apply not only to Portalis's work, especially his famous *Discours préliminaire*, which sets out the aims of the Code, but also to the work of Professor Jean-Louis Halpérin, the author of this work. For Professor Halpérin, who burst on the French academic scene in 1992 with his justly acclaimed *L'impossible code civil*, has combined in his work the talents of a true archival scholar and the arresting eloquence of an experienced journalist conscious of the lack of space. This small book displays both qualities as it traces for the sake of a general reader the birth and early years of the French Civil Code. The emphasis on family and succession law helps contrast the French pre-occupations of the time with the very different emphasis paid by English or Italian law on property, criminology and aspects of contract and commercial law. To the careful reader, it also offers interesting clues on how the French had, by 1799, got tired of the effects of revolutionary excesses and were ready to settle for the calmer (if authoritarian) Napoleonic compromise. This complex strand of thoughts is, in this booklet, presented with the calm authority which stems from a deep knowledge of French history and which, in days gone by, might have been described with three words: *multum in parvo*.

By presenting in English such a scholar and his work – by no means his most esoteric and detailed but by all accounts one of the most popular among French students – we have tried to serve our own student audiences as well as the general reader who would like to know more about the subject of codification. And that is not a bad thing since nowadays the European Commission appears hell-bent to impose on all a European-wide private code under the pretence (exposed by many an authoritative lawyer as spurious) that without it European trade will suffer. Napoleon's encouragement of a compromise document, which involved in its drafting all the major players (not just academics) and expressed the dominant interests of its time in language flexible enough to survive the many upheavals that followed its enactment, must thus be compared with some of the drafts coming out of Northern Europe – heavy in citations, long in detail, cumbersome in expression and proving the accuracy of the Portalis's prophecy that 'one is erudite by the mass of information accumulated but one is wise by the way one uses it'.

Professor Halpérin's work could not have been made usable in England were it not for the efforts of a gifted translator who rendered its meaning and its spirit in flowing English. Finding such a person was not difficult for, in practice, the choice came down to one scholar: Tony Weir. Through his unique talents Mr Weir has thus, once again, rendered a huge service to Anglophone comparatists and reconfirmed his great reputation as a true man of culture. And as if this were not enough, he has provided the reader with a selection of appendices which make the understanding of many of the Revolutionary peculiarities, if not more acceptable, certainly easier to follow.

This volume will be followed by a quick succession of sequels but this is as good an opportunity as any to express our thanks to Mr Sonny Leong, the Director of Cavendish Press, for accepting our suggestion to launch these books as part of his wider publishing agreement with University College London.

Bentham's College, 15 August 2005
Basil Markesinis
Jörg Fedtke

Translator's Foreword

The details of French political history at the end of the eighteenth century may be less familiar to readers of this English version than to the addressees of the original, so with the kind permission of the author, I am appending some factual elucidations.

These additions are located at the end of the book and indicated in the text, and relate to (1) the legislative bodies during the revolutionary period; (2) the political groupings, the Mountain and the Plain; (3) the revolutionary calendar; (4) *état civil*; or the register of births, marriages and deaths; and (5) *majorats*.

Also included is a stylistically very beautiful and concise extract from H.A.L. Fisher's *History of Europe* which gives an English historian's appraisal of Napoleon's contribution to the *Code civil*.

Tony Weir
16 October 2004 (=24 *vendémiaire* year CCXIII)

Chapter 1: The Genesis of the *Code civil*

'A single body of law, called the *Code civil* is to be created.' So proclaimed the Law of 21 March 1804 (30 *ventôse* year XII). It was to be created by the amalgamation of 36 texts recently adopted. This was the culmination of an enterprise started many years previously. The idea of unifying the French private law, conceived under Louis XI, had been frequently repeated since then, but under the *ancien régime* lawyers never got beyond sketching and planning. Proper drafts of a civil code were put to assembly after assembly under the Revolution, but in 10 years none of them was ever adopted. The attempts to put the idea into practice is documented in the following section. The four years of the Consulate were more favourable to the production and adoption of a civil code – with the arrival of Bonaparte and the end of the Revolution the time had come for action, and the private law of France was finally codified (Section 2).

Section 1: Visions and projects

The word 'code' comes from the Latin *codex*, denoting a book consisting of tablets or pages bound together. In the closing centuries of the Roman Empire books in this form replaced scrolls, and were particularly useful for works on law since scrolls had to be unrolled in order to be consulted. *The Code of Theodosius* (438) and the *Byzantine Code of Justinian* (534) were official collections of imperial constitutions, replacing earlier private compilations. Justinian's Code, whose 12 books contained five centuries of imperial legislation on private law, criminal law and public law, was unrivalled as a source of law for hundreds of years, so people came to think of a 'code' as denoting a collection of legislation from which it became relatively easy to ascertain what the law was.

In the *ancien droit* which obtained in France after the turn of the millennium no such idea was current. The legislative power of the king virtually disappeared during the feudal period, and private law depended on custom (*coutume*). When Justinian's Code was rediscovered in the twelfth-century France did not 'receive' it as national law: in other European countries 'codification' came to mean a way of transforming the *ius commune* based on Roman law, but not in France. It is true that in the final centuries of the *ancien régime* there were aspirations for a single law for the whole of France under the authority of the King (I), but during the Revolution people were much more interested in using legislation as a means of social engineering (II).

I. The desire for uniformity in the ancien régime

From the sixteenth to the eighteenth centuries French private law was very different in the various parts of the country. In northern and central France there were as many as 65 general customs in force, as well as over 300 local customs, often differing from them in detail. Most of these customs were put into writing in the sixteenth century, whereas the South was always the land of *droit écrit*. There the law was Roman, as modified by local conditions and the decisions of the local *Parlement*. Both major systems of law were supplemented throughout the kingdom by canon law, which applied to certain matters such as marriage, and also, especially in the area of the law of obligations, by Roman law in the guise of 'written reason'. There was additional input from writers and courts. In theory all this law was applicable by way of royal concession, on the view that the king had a monopoly of legislative power and could in principle make any laws he pleased for private citizens.

As the feeling of nationhood grew, so did the idea of replacing the existing variety of laws by a single private law, possibly a code, common to all of France, but this was something the monarchy was reluctant to undertake (A), and the jurists themselves were not very active in the matter (B).

A. The monarchy is reluctant

The eighteenth century saw the first wave of codification in Europe. Collections of laws were published in Piedmont-Sardinia (1723), and Bavaria produced a civil code in 1756. Reform in Prussia was stimulated by Frederick II. A first draft, published in 1749–51 and translated into French, was followed in 1780–86 by a redraft produced by Chancellor Carmer with the assistance of the jurists Suarez and Klein, and the *Allgemeines Landrecht* was finally published in 1794. It is a general code of more than 19,000 articles, covering not only private law but criminal law, feudal law and the law of the church as well.

In comparison with this exciting programme of codification in Europe the French monarchy seems to have achieved but little in the area of private law. Royal ordinances had admittedly increased in number since the sixteenth century, but they only rarely affected private law, and then only on particular points. For example, the great reforming Ordinance of Blois contained 363 articles, but only five of them touched on matrimony. When Daguesseau was Chancellor he had a real plan for legislation in private law, but it was only very partially brought to fruition. His ultimate aim was to produce a 'sort of code', or more realistically a series of texts summarising the case law, and he did actually produce three important ordinances on donations (1731), wills (1735) and substitutions (1747) which applied alike in the areas of customary law and in the lands of *droit écrit*. His plans to extend this work to include intestate succession and obligations had to be abandoned, however, and his successors were even less daring.

In the second half of the eighteenth century the King's counsellors sketched out rather simple plans for a code, but that was all. In 1759 Laverdy (later controller general of finances between 1763 and 1768) and Langlois, both magistrates and counsellors at the *Parlement de Paris*, produced a plan to unify the customs, excepting 'rules which were wholly incompatible', and in 1771 Chancellor Maupeou considered harmonising some of the customs whose rules were 'unduly divergent', but his work on the Custom of Normandy proved abortive. Finally, in 1778, in deference to the King's desire to simplify and harmonise the customs, the Minister of Justice, Lamoignon, created a Full Court and tasked it to produce a single consistent register of royal legislation.

The monarchy lacked the political will to go any further. Traditionally Kings intervened little in private law – the law which 'concerns individuals' – and even the *Code Louis*, as the great ordinances initiated by Colbert under Louis XIV were sometimes called, dealt only with topics of direct concern to the state and the system of justice – procedure (civil in 1667 and criminal in 1670), commerce, maritime matters, the colonies, and inland waterways and forests. In other areas, such as family law, property law (where feudalism caused difficulties) and even contracts, the King preferred to allow each territory to keep its own law, whether customary or Romanesque. It was generally thought that the provinces had been 'granted to France on condition that their laws and customs be maintained' (Auzarin), and it was not for royalty to subvert the structures of a society founded on privileges, which are, after all, intrinsically incompatible with the idea of a law common to all.

This refusal to try to unify private law from above distinguishes the French monarchy from the 'enlightened despotism' of the Age of Reason. The Kings of France had no intention of forcing the people to adopt a law common to all, by imposing one custom rather than another or by drawing on Roman law, which was still regarded as rather foreign. Having had difficulties enough in introducing reforms of a fiscal or procedural nature they were by no means eager to add a further ground of dissension by introducing 'disturbing novelties' into private law and would certainly have endorsed Montesquieu's view that 'citizens should obey the law, but not necessarily the same law'. The *Parlements* likewise kept saying that 'the king's justice must vary from territory to territory'.

B. The lawyers are diffident

The lawyers could not of course legislate – only the King could do that – but they might have advanced the cause of unification by the means at their disposal. Although the practitioners of customary law tended to concentrate on the law of their own province, there had been signs as early as the sixteenth century, in the wake of isolated precursors such as Dumoulin and Hotman, of a desire to unify it. In works called *conférences* or *agrégatoires* some jurists attempted to elicit a 'common customary law' by comparing the various customs, preference often being given to the Custom of Paris. Lamoignon, President of the *Parlement de Paris* under Louis XIV, drafted a set of articles with a view to 'reducing all the customs to a single custom', but this private enterprise was unsuccessful – Lamoignon himself recognising that the customs were so diverse that it was rarely possible to find a single principle common to them all, much less to harmonise them with the *droit écrit*.

Others believed that the law of reason could serve as a model for the entire kingdom. Domat's *Lois civiles dans leur ordre naturel* (1689–94) is an example: in addition to setting out the law applied in his native Clermont, an enclave of *droit écrit* in the Auvergne (otherwise largely customary), he sought to record in a single book and 'in a simple and natural order' all the current maxims of private law, drawing on Roman law as a source of legal science and reason. Fifty or so years later, the works of Pothier (1699–1772), the most famous holder of any of the chairs of 'French law' established in 1679, dealt with the Customs of Orléans and Paris alongside Roman law, and Bourjon's *Le droit commun de la France et la coutume de Paris réduits en principe* (1747) did for the Custom of Paris what Domat had done for Roman law. The novel method of presentation of these works helped to clarify the existing law but did not really modify its actual substance, and their authors failed to suggest any practical method of unifying the private law of France. The possibility of codification was never even mentioned.

In the final decades of the *ancien régime* most lawyers just wrote commentaries on customary law or on the *droit écrit*, often observing that the differences were so great that it was impossible to create a rational national law. But if this conservative scepticism was predominant, there were a few lawyers who were less traditionally minded. In 1771, for example, Guyton de Morveau, *avocat-général* in the *Parlement* of Burgundy, tried to galvanise the jurists by proposing that a commission of lawyers produce 20 chapters of principles for the king to render authoritative 'after mature reflection'. More radically, Linguet castigated the archaic patchwork of private law (*Théorie des lois civiles*, 1767) and proposed a thorough recension of private law, modelled on the law of the sultans, and in the 1770s we find practitioners increasingly demanding reform and criticising the 'barbarity' of the customs.

Meanwhile philosophers such as Diderot (who offered advice on legislation to Catherine II) and Rousseau (*Considérations sur le gouvernment de Pologne*, 1772) were promoting the idea of codification which Montesquieu (*Esprit des lois*, book 28, chapter 37) had treated so very coolly. The code they envisaged was not to be a mere compilation of existing laws but an integrated whole, presenting a brand-new law adapted to the spirit of the age in a clear, brief and precise manner, sometimes even proposing to abolish primogeniture and introduce divorce.

Two lawyers in the 1780s produced works which can be regarded as private drafts of a *Code civil*, though they are not articulated as such. In *Les lois civiles et l'administration de la justice* (1782–83) Pétion wrote in favour of allowing divorce and granting a right of inheritance to all legitimate children except married daughters, and even (if there were no legitimate children) illegitimate offspring. In 1788 a book with somewhat less radical proposals for reform was put forward by Picard de Prébois: it bore the prophetic title *Introduction à un seul code de lois*.

II. The Revolution's ambitious projects

In early 1789 expressions of a desire for unified law (alongside statements of a preference for local laws) figure in the *cahiers de doléances* or lists of grievances submitted by the local delegations to the *États-généraux*, a body which quickly gave way to the *Assemblée nationale constituante* (see below p. 97). The *Constituante* proceeded to abolish privileges (4 August 1789) and promulgate the Declaration of the Rights of Man and Citizen (26 August 1789), thereby heralding a new concept of law, omniscient and uniform. The members of the *Constituante* were largely in favour of using legislation as a means of revitalising the nation including codifying private law. Mirabeau was much impressed by the codification process in Prussia, and Siéyès's definition of a nation was of 'a body of members living under a common law and represented by a single legislature'. The current distinction between political and civil rights suggested that there should be both a constitution and a code of private law, and indeed the Constitution of 1791, echoing an article from the Judiciary Law of 16–24 August 1790, started out by laying down that '[T]here shall be a code of private law common to the whole kingdom'.

The Revolution of 1789 certainly did away with some of the obstacles to the codification of private law which had existed under the *ancien régime*, but there were still difficulties in the way of its achievement. The *Constituante* regarded it as more important to reform criminal law than to produce a civil code, so the first code to see the light of day in France was the *Code pénal* of 1791. The members of the *Constituante* did not even discuss the drafts on private law which were put before them, such as the *Nouveau Code civil* of Olivier from Avignon (in the form of articles) and the *Projet de législation civile* by Philippeaux, both of which were in line with the attempts under the *ancien régime* to unify the *Coutume de Paris* with the Roman law. It was perhaps wise to be cautious in dealing with controversial subjects such as marriage and succession – the law of 8–14 April 1791, which required legitimate children to be treated equally, did not alter the amount of property of which the decedent was free to dispose (*quotité disponible*), and though marriage was to be treated as merely a civil contract (as it had been already in the Constitution of 1791) it was not until the final session of the *Assemblée législative* on 20 September 1792 that divorce was introduced and the law of personal status reorganised. The *Convention* which succeeded the *Assemblée* did consider official proposals for a code, but despite their revolutionary flavour they were unsuccessful (A), and no greater success attended the less radical proposals put forward as revolutionary fervour waned (B).

A. The radical Convention

The *Montagnards* among the deputies, passionately devoted to the indivisibility of the republic as against the 'hydra' of federalism endorsed by the Girondins, now proscribed (see below p. 101), wanted a civil law which was uniform and egalitarian, and on 9 August 1793 after the adoption of the Constitution of 1791 Cambacérès, as president of the legislative committee, put before the *Convention* and submitted for popular approval a project for a civil code. It had been prepared in two months by a committee of 12 lawyers, including specialists in private law such as Berlier, Oudot, Garran-Coulon and Merlin of Douai (working under Cambacérès), whose official task was to reform the law of securities, and using a library containing works by the *philosophes* of the Enlightenment as well as earlier jurists.

This, the first of Cambacérès's projects, purported to be building 'on the terra firma of the law of nature and the virgin soil of the Republic'. Lean and mean, its mere 791 Arts rejected prior law almost *in toto*. It endorsed the principles of the two laws of 20 September 1792 on personal status and divorce (no ground needing to be stated), and abolished the power of husband and father: the administration of household property was to be shared between the spouses, whose only duty to the children was to educate and protect them until they were 21. Anyone, married or not, could adopt a minor, illegitimate children voluntarily recognised by their father were to have the same rights of succession as legitimate children, and strict equality was to be observed among children, none to be preferred to others and no gifts to be made to those already wealthy enough. The purpose of all this was to 'break up large estates'. By contrast with these radical innovations in family law, the proposals relating to property and obligations came largely from prior law, subject to the abolition of feudal rights, but ownership was defined as 'the right of the owner to enjoy and dispose of it' (as under the Declaration of Rights of 1790), and the freedom to contract, to acquire and to dispose of property was entrenched.

In August and September 1793 the *Convention* discussed Books One and Two of the draft (personal status and property); it endorsed most of the texts but adjourned others. In October it went against the wishes of Cambacérès in deciding that the principle of equal rights on succession should be applied retrospectively to all cases arising after 14 July 1789 (the fall of the Bastille), but adoption of the text still seemed imminent when on 3 November 1793 the *Convention* deferred further discussion *sine die* and voted to remit the project to a commission of 'six philosophers'. The ostensible ground was that a civil code should be 'purged' of legalistic prejudices, but the truth was that since the members of the *Convention* had just suspended the Constitution and set up a revolutionary government, the adoption of a civil code was no longer politically appropriate. The only parts enacted were the two retrospective laws of 2 November 1793 and 6 January 1794 (12 *brumaire* and 17 *nîvose* year II) relating to illegitimate children and successions.

The commission of 'philosophers' never met, but the legislative committee set to work again, probably in the Spring of 1794, and produced a further draft which Cambacérès submitted to the *Convention* on 9 September 1794 (23 *fructidor* Year II). This text was very laconic, only 297 articles long, not only shorter than its predecessor but also modified in the light of the reservations of the legislative committee. Cambacérès's report sought to justify this supposed 'code of nature' by a rather paradoxical reference to Lockean 'liberal' philosophy: 'All civil rights rest on freedom of liberty, property and contract.' In December 1794 the *Convention* discussed 10 of these articles but then abandoned the matter as inconsistent with its aims, for in the 'reaction to Thermidor' it was now ready to reconsider the enthusiasms of the Revolution. The *Convention* broke up in October 1795 without adopting a civil code, but only a law on mortgages and one on crimes and penalties.

B. The more moderate Directory

Cambacérès, however, was as determined as ever to have a civil code, and at the beginning of the Directory in June 1796 he and a few collaborators, including Oudot and Berlier, produced a third draft. The 1794 idea of a 'collection of maxims' was now abandoned, and the 1,104 articles of this third draft drew openly on Roman law, pre-Revolutionary law and Pothier. In his introductory remarks Cambacérès tried to give the impression that he was being true to the principles of the various laws he cited, but in fact he emphasised marriage as being 'of the first importance to society' in order to placate the many people who found the revolutionary legislation 'immoral'.

Not all the innovations of the Revolution were discarded: divorce remained available in accordance with the Law of 1792, subject to 'adjustments' proposed by Cambacérès, the adoption of minors remained possible in principle and equality was still to be strictly observed in the succession of legitimate children. Nevertheless there were certain important differences: only persons with no children of their own could adopt, women married under the statutory matrimonial property regime were incapable, testators without children were allowed to dispose of more of their estate than under the Law of 6 January 1794 (17 *nivôse* year II), and adopted children were entitled to only half as much as legitimate children, as were illegitimate children, if recognised after marriage. The law of property and contracts was treated in greater detail and the underlying principles were stated more clearly: 'the owner has the right to enjoy and dispose of his property as he chooses, subject to laws established for the needs of the community' (Art 415), and 'every contract, of whatever nature, is law between the parties to it' (Art 714).

In December 1796 Cambacérès did his best to move the discussion of his draft forward, but the Council of Five Hundred temporised and in the Assembly where more reactionary proposals regarding illegitimate children and divorce were ventilated, only two of his articles were adopted. In February 1797 when Cambacérès last spoke on the subject, he conceded that the draft should be sent back for reconsideration. He was quite right to scuttle the project, for the chances of success were virtually nil: in the following spring, indeed, he himself failed to be re-elected. This was the third time Cambacérès fell victim to a political situation unfavourable to his aims – the revolutionary assemblies were perfectly capable of adopting major radical laws but they failed to adopt a civil code which would fix relations between citizens and within the family for the future, and later when the pendulum swung back after the fall of Robespierre it proved impossible to reconcile the views then current with the fervour of 1792–94.

In 1799 when the Directory was reaching its end the very idea of codification was put on the back burner, despite the reemergence of Cambacérès as Minister of Justice. People were becoming more sceptical as the swings of politics seemed to imperil the very stability of the Republic, and some, such as Portalis in 1797, even doubted whether a civil code could be produced at all. Others, however, including the lawyers Jacqueminot and Target, returned to the task of drafting a project. Rather than 'making a civil code in one fell swoop' the former preferred to set out 'elementary principles' on the more delicate aspects of family law. Target's draft of 272 articles was more ambitious, but was never even published.

In view of its date – it was produced in December 1799 during the provisional Consulate just after the coup d'État of 9 November 1799 (8 *brumaire* VIII) – Jacqueminot's draft can be considered as the final revolutionary attempt to produce a code. The texts of Jacqueminot and Target were alike in many respects, putting an end to 'the scandal of incessant divorces', retaining the incapacity of the wife, reducing the portion of illegitimate children, and restoring to fathers 'the legitimate power they should never have lost'. Jacqueminot was also minded to prohibit gifts between man and mistress. These views mark the transition in reaction to Thermidor from the enthusiasms of the Revolution to the realism of the Consulate.

Section 2: The *Code civil* is drafted

The ink was hardly dry on the Constitution of 1799 when Jacqueminot announced that pursuant to 'the wishes and the provident wisdom of the great man' who just a few weeks previously had become Head of the State a civil code was to be enacted. Ever since the beginning of the Consulate, Bonaparte meant to have legislation bearing his name reflect the aims of his regime to bring the Revolution to a close while maintaining most of its achievements, to reinforce and reconstruct the fabric of society, and to increase the power of the state by unifying it and centralising the administration. A successful civil code could be highly advantageous to him personally, giving him the prestige of a lawmaker, helping to concentrate his hold on power, and enhancing the glory of his military successes.

Bonaparte's support was not the only feature in the situation favourable to the creation of a civil code: the currency was stabilising, the economy was improving, religion was reintroduced by the Concordat of 1801, there was peace both at home and, from 1802 to 1804, abroad, and the assemblies with their ideological factions were in decline; all of this conduced to the enactment of a civil code, and furthermore lawyers trained under the *ancien régime* had returned and were on hand to produce a draft which could generate support and satisfy Bonaparte, himself (I). To an extent quite exceptional for a head of state he took part in the examination of the text, alternating debate and direction (II). On the technical aspects of the draftsmanship he doubtless had less influence (III), but such is the connection between form and substance that he may well be considered as not just the facilitator but actually one of the authors of the Code (see below p. 109).

I. The production of the draft

On 12 August 1800 (24 *thermidor* year VIII) Bonaparte appointed a committee of four members to lay the foundations for civil legislation. The work of his nominees, characteristically appointed without consulting the assemblies, was so effective that it has become normal to treat them as the actual draftsmen of the *Code civil* (A), but while the draft they produced at the end of the year is unquestionably the matrix of the Code, there are a number of important points on which the eventual text nevertheless diverges from it (B).

A. The four draftsmen

The president of the committee, the senior and probably the best-known of the four members, was Tronchet (1726–1806). As early as 1745, he had been an *avocat* at the *Parlement de Paris* and was Head of the Bar there in 1789. As a delegate of the third estate in the *États-généraux*, unhappy at its transformation into the *Constituante*, he sided with the monarchists and helped decide which feudal rights were to be suppressed and which subject to commutation. Under the Directory he served again as a deputy and member of the *Conseil des Anciens* 1795–98, while ostensibly keeping clear of party squabbles. At the start of the Consulate he became president of the *tribunal de cassation*, which confirmed his reputation as a specialist.

If Tronchet was the sophisticated expert in pre-Revolutionary law and a notable defender of the *Coutume de Paris*, Portalis (1746–1807) stands out as the 'philosopher' of the committee. After a brilliant career as an advocate in Aix he joined the monarchist party under the Revolution, was blacklisted as an émigré in 1792, had to take refuge in Lyons, and was briefly imprisoned. After the elections of 1795 he joined the *Conseil des Anciens* and proved so effective a speaker for the 'constitutional' royalists that he was deported under the law of 5 September 1797 (19 *fructidor* V). The intellectual contacts he made during his exile in Switzerland and Germany helped develop his legal thinking, and when Bonaparte allowed him to return to France he became *commissaire du gouvernement* in the Prize Council.

Bigot de Préameneu (1747–1825) started out as advocate at the *Parlement de Rennes*, established himself in Paris, and got to know Portalis when he was general agent of the *États* of Provence. He served as judge under the *Constituante* and the Directory, sat on the side of the defenders of Louis XVI, and was imprisoned under the Terror. Under the

Consulate he became *commissaire du gouvernement* at the *tribunal de cassation*.

Maleville (1741–1824), the secretary of the committee to begin with, had been an advocate in the *Parlement* of Bordeaux and then judge on the *tribunal de cassation* (1791–95) to which he returned after a period as member of the *Conseil des Anciens*.

The careers and opinions of the four men were broadly similar: they had all practised as lawyers either under customary law or the *droit écrit*, were experienced parliamentarians, and were fundamentally moderate and disinclined to revolutionise the law. The work was divided between them but they had no difficulty in coming to agreement without losing their individuality.

B. The draft of 1801

Although it is called the 'Draft of year VIII' in the *Recueil Fenet*, the text which the committee had worked on for five months was actually printed on 1 *pluviôse* year IX (21 January 1801). Many features of the future *Code civil* appear in its three books: the secular nature of civil status and marriage, the incapacity of married women, the reinstatement of strong paternal power ending with emancipation on majority, the distinction between legitimate and illegitimate children, and the confirmation of 'full' ownership of property and freedom of contract. After a preliminary title referring to 'universal and immutable law', characteristic features were that divorce was to be available only for stated causes, the disposable part of an estate where there were dependants was fixed at one-quarter, in line with the recent law of 25 March 1800 (4 *germinal* year VIII), and a provision whereby the part of a spendthrift heir could be reduced to a life interest with remainder to his children (*disposition officieuse*). There was no reference at all to adoption, the role of the dowry regime of matrimonial property was reduced and a system of general and unregistered mortgages was introduced.

The famous *Discours préliminaire* which introduced the draft was written by Portalis but is thought to represent the views of all the members of the committee. It begins by showing that while codification had been impossible not only under the *ancien régime*, when France was merely a network of groups, but also under the Revolution, when the laws were 'hostile, discriminatory and divisive', it was at last possible now that 'France can draw breath'. It proceeds to state that legislation should be imbued with a 'philosophy of moderation': the legislator must be 'sparing with innovations', profit from the experience of the past (by effecting a compromise between the *droit écrit* and the customs) and resist any 'desire to regulate and provide for every eventuality'. Self-restraint on the part of the lawgiver would increase the importance of the courts and enhance the role of lawyers, because 'one can no more do without decisions than without laws' and 'it takes time to make codes for peoples, if indeed they can be said to be made at all'. Finally, it stated that private law 'under the guardianship of political laws' is fully justified if adapted to the customs of the people and designed to further 'family spirit'.

II. The discussion of the draft

The publication of the draft triggered a major debate, which the First Consul sought to control at every stage. In order to reconcile the legal profession to the codification the views of the courts were sought (A), the *Conseil d'État* played a critical role in rewriting the draft (B) and the assemblies which showed signs of being difficult were quickly reduced to the role of a rubberstamp (C).

A. The views of the courts

Most of the observations came from the five members nominated by the *tribunal de cassation* to examine the draft. A majority regretted the absence of adoption and suggested that subject to special tests divorce should be available even if no specific ground were offered. They also wanted to see disinherison re-established within 'sensible limits' and suggested a new system for recording special mortgages. It is clear that opinion among the top judges was seriously divided, especially on divorce and equality in succession, and that some of them remained attached to certain features of the revolutionary laws.

The courts of appeal were very largely hostile to any extension of divorce, and split mainly on questions of the matrimonial regime and succession. Montpellier protested vigorously against the very modest place attributed to the dowry, a point on which the courts of Toulouse, Bordeaux and Aix remained silent. In parts of the country previously under customary law there was a majority in favour of equality in succession, whereas the courts in the South, and also Paris, wanted to see an increase in the disposable portion. By and large, however, the judges quite liked the temper of the government's draft.

B. Discussion in the Conseil d'État

Under the Constitution of 1799 the *Conseil d'État* had a crucial role in the reforms of the Consulate, for its task was to draft bills which only the government could propose. Bonaparte had filled it with experienced lawyers, men such as Berlier, Boulay de la Meurthe, Emmery, Regnault de Saint-Jean-d'Angély and Thibaudeau, whose careers under the Revolution had been quite varied. The legislative section examined the draft Civil Code in private, starting on 17 July 1801 (28 *messidor* year IX), and proposed a number of amendments. It was then discussed in plenary session from September 1801 to 1803. The proceedings of the 107 meetings are known to us not only from the official minutes but also from the testimony of witnesses, so we know that Bonaparte himself presided at 55 of those meetings and took an active part in the discussions, during which he allowed the members to state their opinions freely. Cambacérès, as Second Consul, was also very much present.

The four draftsmen defended their text, but significant modifications were made. To begin with, Portalis was required by the legislative section to withdraw his preliminary book and substitute a very short and simple title. When divorce was debated in September 1801, Bonaparte and several of the counsellors regretted that the draft did not permit divorce for incompatibility of temperament, but thanks to Emmery and Boulay de la Meurthe a compromise formula was found: divorce could be by mutual consent, whether due to mutual incompatibility or unadmitted fault. As to adoption, Bonaparte – backed by Berlier – used his influence to have it reintroduced, but the text had to go through six drafts before it was finally adopted in January 1803 (*nîvose* year XI). Not until 1803–04 was compromise finally reached on the question of how much of his property a testator could dispose of if he wished – the amount was to vary depending on the number of children – and on matrimonial property regimes (more detail being added to the part dealing with the dowry regime).

On many issues, therefore, the discussions in the *Conseil d'État* were of crucial importance. From them we learn of Bonaparte's own opinions on certain issues, resulting in part from his personal family arrangements, and of the divergence of views among the members of the committee (Portalis, for example, disliked the statutory regime of community property). We also see that the controversies of the revolutionary era survived into the ideological climate of the Consulate.

C. Discussion in the assemblies curtailed

Under the Constitution of 1799 the governmental draft of the Code had to be submitted to two assemblies: the Tribunate, whose members could speak for or against the proposal, and the Legislative Body, which had to listen in silence to speakers from the Tribunate and the *Conseil d'État*, and could then only adopt or reject the draft. This procedure started in late 1801 after the text, now divided up into several separate bills, had been put in final form by the *Conseil d'État*.

Bonaparte's political opponents, who had been fairly muted during the first two years of the Consulate, now began to express themselves more forcibly, and the atmosphere in the Tribunate, where proper discussion was possible, was rather tense – many of its members having been upset by the signature of the Concordat some months previously.

The preliminary title was vigorously attacked, and the Tribunate voted against it by 65 to 13. According to Andrieux, Chazal, Garat-Mailla, Thiessé and Favard it was 'incoherent', had no place at the forefront of a civil code, and in any case gave too much power to the judges when the law was silent; furthermore, it confused promulgation with publication. These arguments suggested that the draftsmen were simply incompetent and persuaded a bare majority of the Legislative Body to reject the draft by 142 votes to 139. The title on the exercise and deprivation of civil rights was then attacked by Boissy d'Anglas, Ganilh (who favoured the rights of foreigners) and M.-J. Chénier, who demanded a civil code 'free from the gothic prejudices which had been confuted by philosophy'. The Tribunate's vote on 1 January 1802 (11 *nivôse* X) was unfavourable (61 votes to 11). Meanwhile, the Tribunate had approved the title on the documentation on personal status despite the criticisms of Benjamin Constant. In fact the Tribunate was not really opposed to the idea of codification as such or even to the main lines of the government's draft but was seizing on formal infelicities so as to assert its right to criticise it freely, an attitude Bonaparte took as a personal affront. He withdrew all the drafts, deprived the assemblies of legislative business (*diète des lois*), and took the first opportunity on 20 March 1802 (29 *ventôse* year X) to exclude the most outspoken opponents. After this purge the assemblies became docile and the several bills constituting the Civil Code were voted in by large majorities, with the Tribunate merely suggesting a few amendments.

III. The drafting technique

Despite its scrutiny in draft by several deliberative groups the *Code civil* remains quite consistent in style and structure, owing much to the projects of Cambacérès and to the views of the draftsmen that a code should be open (A) and systematic (B).

A. An open-textured Code?

Although Portalis agreed with Cambacérès that legislation need not try to cover everything and that one of the aims of codification was to simplify the law applicable to individuals, the *Code civil* with its 2,281 articles is much longer than any of the revolutionary drafts. Unlike the Prussian Code of 1794 the *Code civil* has no general part on civil rights and acts-in-law: having abandoned the idea of a preliminary book on the law the draftsmen favoured the practical over the scientific. Rather than get involved in doctrinal detail or casuistry, they sought to find a suitable language (using the present or future indicative rather than the imperative). The Code contains hardly any principles of philosophy or morals (even Art 371 – 'Throughout his life a child must honour and respect his parents' – is legally meaningful) and does not overindulge in definitions (for example, 'marriage' and 'obligation' remain undefined).

In the belief that matters of detail were for lawyers and courts, the draftsmen left a lot of room for development by case law. 'Regulatory decisions' are certainly prohibited by Art 5, but under Art 4 the judge must decide the case before him even if the law is obscure or deficient. Portalis's view that judges were 'ministers of equity' can be traced in several provisions (for example Arts 565, 1135 and 1854). Even more important is the role left to custom, especially on topics such as the use of rivers, woods, the distances to be left between buildings and fences, and agricultural leases. The Code is by no means introverted.

B. A systematic Code?

Although, rather surprisingly, Cambacérès was ready to leave several different laws in force, the draftsmen unhesitatingly decided, in line with the desire for uniformity which had been constant throughout the period from 1789 to 1804, to revoke all previous law on the topics covered by the Code (Law of 21 March 1804; 30 *ventôse* year XII). Customary law, Roman law and royal ordinances ceased to be binding, or even persuasive, though the judge could resort to them if the law were silent. The *Code civil* is thus the first European code to abolish all previous law, for while the Prussian Code of 1794 displaced the suppletive *ius commune*, provincial customs and city laws remained valid. The *Code civil* was also novel in numbering its articles sequentially, thereby showing that it was a single law and not a mere collection.

Another difference between the Prussian Code and the *Code civil* is that the latter, like the drafts of Cambacérès, is concerned exclusively with private law, that is, the rules which regulate the relations of individuals with each other. Distinguished from public law (see Art 7 on the exercise of 'civil rights') this law covered all private relations in national society, commercial law being treated as exceptional. This strict delimitation of the coverage of the Code gives it its unity, though of course there are internal divisions, for the Code is divided into three books of unequal length ('On Persons,' Arts 1–515, 'On Property and its Variants,' Arts 516–710, and 'On the Different Modes of Acquiring Property,' Arts 711–2281). The draftsmen did not claim that their division was original, elegant or scientifically precise, but merely reflected the 'common divisions', as they themselves said. Nor did they conceal the fact that the *Code civil* was a system which turned on two axes – the family and property – which will be the subject of the following chapters.

Chapter 2: Law for Fathers

The *Discours préliminaire* concludes by stating that the aim of the draftsmen was to 'bring law and social behaviour into harmony and to promote family feeling, which, whatever one may say, conduces so greatly to the sense of citizenship'. The word 'family' does not actually appear as such in the titles of the divisions of the Code, but the family nevertheless, as Portalis said, constitutes one of the 'two solid foundations' of the body of law designed to 'promote and stabilise social relations'. The individual cannot be apprehended in isolation: his personal status is status within the family, the 'nursery' of the state. Book One of the Code is entitled '*Of persons*' but one should not be misled: it is not like the book of the same name in the Prussian Code, which contains a series of definitions on the rights of persons generally, for here the family is omnipresent in the background throughout the four opening titles on civil rights, the documentation of civil status, domicile and missing persons (Section 1). The next seven titles, beginning with marriage, are manifestly concerned with relations between members of the family (Section 2), and the provisions on matrimonial property and succession, which are admittedly placed in Book Three, are logically considered here, since they concern property relations within the family (Section 3).

Section 1: The individual and the family

Title I of Book One of the *Code civil* opens by drawing a fundamental distinction between *civil rights*, to be defined in what follows, and *political rights*, the subject of constitutional law. While the Constitution determines whether or not one is a French citizen, the *Code civil* deals with what that entails and how the citizen's civil rights are protected (I). Since, as Bonaparte said, 'what a man does is hardly ever determined by his volition alone', the law treats each person from birth to death according to his civil status (II).

I. Who has civil rights?

The upsurge in national feeling and the extent of emigration during the ten years of the Revolution meant that the codifiers had to face tricky questions when deciding what rules to lay down regarding the exercise of civil rights. The provisions on being French (A) and the loss of civil rights (B) are consequently rather a mixture of principle and pragmatism.

A. Being French

Since '[A]ll French people enjoy civil rights' (Art 8), the Code has to say how one becomes French. Full civil rights are, as a general rule, conferred on those 'born to a Frenchman' either in France or abroad (Art 10). Nationality (a word not yet in use at the time) is transmitted within the family, with a preponderant role being played by the father, whose wife takes the status of her husband (Arts 12 and 19). An individual born in France to a foreign parent becomes French only if he claims this status within a year of reaching the age of majority and fixes his domicile in France (in such a case the Constitution of 1799 – year VIII – allowed a man aged 21 to become a citizen). The *Code civil* here adopts the old principle of *ius sanguinis* as against Bonaparte's preference for the *ius soli*.

Foreigners on French soil are subject to the rules of the police and public order (Art 3), and have such civil rights as their nation accords to French people (Art 11), a clause of reciprocity which went some way towards re-establishing the *droit d'aubaine* in matters of succession. A foreigner enjoyed full civil rights only if the government had granted him the right of domicile (Art 13). The codifiers, unlike the *Constituante*, were trying to protect French capital against nations such as the English.

B. Loss of civil rights

Civil rights were lost when one ceased to be French. If one established oneself abroad with no intention of returning (with a notable exception for businessmen), was naturalised in a foreign country, or accepted public office abroad without authorisation (Art 17) this was taken to indicate abdication of French nationality. In sanctioning French citizens who served another government, especially in the army, the codifiers clearly had in mind the *émigrés* who took up arms against the Revolution. French citizenship could generally be recovered on returning to France with the authorisation of the Head of State (Art 18), but anyone who had served in a foreign army was subject to all the conditions imposed on foreigners who wished to become French citizens (Art 21). The children of *émigrés* born abroad were treated more leniently (Art 10).

Civil death, as Portalis and Tronchet rather ambiguously called it, is the other ground on which one could be deprived of one's civil rights. This occurred on conviction of certain offences and, in principle, on emigration (under Art 93 of the Constitution of 1799 and, for those who took up arms against France, Art 21 of the *Code civil*). The Criminal

Code of 1808 was to provide for the civil death of those condemned to hard labour for life, deportation or the guillotine (only the latter two cases having been covered under the Revolution).

Civil death put an end to the convict's marriage and his property rights (Art 25). The state seems to benefit more from this than the family. The succession of the person civilly dead was admittedly opened in favour of his heirs, but any acquisitions thereafter fell forfeit to the state when he actually did die, and the dissolution of his marriage, which Bonaparte disapproved of, might well be contrary to the wishes of a faithful spouse. By omitting to mention *émigrés* specifically, the Code effectively reinforced the amnesties favoured by Bonaparte, notably by the senatus-consultum of 27 March 1802 (6 *germinal* year X).

II. Civil status

Title II of Book One of the *Code civil* restates the principle of the secularisation of civil status (see below p. 105) and ratifies most of the rules laid down by the Law of 20–25 September 1792, with the striking exception of the competence of women to serve as witnesses (Art 37). In implicit confirmation of the Law of 17 February 1800 (28 *pluviôse* VIII) mayors and local officials were to keep the register of births, marriages and deaths. The rules on civil status and their supervision by the state were designed to 'keep the family together and separate from other families', special attention being paid to questions of parentage. Siméon quoted the *Digest* of Justinian in support of his view that the individual 'is not born for himself alone nor even for his family, but for the state' – a view reflected in the topics treated in the following two sections, domicile (A) and missing persons (B).

A. Domicile

Every person's domicile, defined as the place of his 'principal establishment' (Art 102), must be fixed so as to 'preserve social order' (Emmery) and facilitate the service of judicial proceedings. Men of full age and unmarried women were in principle free to come and go as they pleased, subject only to notifying the authorities of any change of domicile. By contrast, those who were not 'free to dispose of their persons' – that is, minors, married women and persons under interdict – necessarily took the domicile of father, husband or tutor respectively. This kept the family together.

B. Absence

Since more and more people were travelling, on business or otherwise, without leaving word of their whereabouts, the codifiers devised clear and formal rules about missing persons, those who 'in the eyes of the law are neither alive nor dead'. If a person had been absent for five years the court, after inquiring into the circumstances, could send the heirs into temporary possession of the estate, which became definitive after thirty years. This was in the interests of the missing person and his family. The missing person was not presumed dead until a hundred years after his birth (Art 129); the spouse could remarry in the meantime, but at the risk of having the marriage avoided should the husband miraculously reappear.

Section 2: Relationships within the family

In the view of the codifiers, the family, 'the most natural of associations', is established by marriage (I), and since its aim is the procreation of children, Book One proceeds quite logically to deal with parentage (II) and then with paternal power and guardianship (III).

I. Marriage reinstated, divorce tolerated

In order to restore to marriage the 'dignity' which it had lost during the Revolution, the codifiers emphasised its nature as 'the most holy of undertakings' (A), reaffirmed the dominance of the husband in the conjugal relationship (B) and made it more difficult to obtain a divorce (C).

A. Marriage – a contract under family and state control

Marriage is not defined in the *Code civil* but Portalis described it as 'the association of man and woman who join together to perpetuate the human race, to help each other bear the burdens of life, and to share their common destiny'. It is a solemn contract in line with the principles of the Law of 20 September 1792, but despite resting on the consent of the parties (Art 180; Portalis spoke of 'choice', 'preference' and even of 'love') one of its functions is to 'restrain the passions of man'. The requirements and formalities of marriage are laid down in Arts 144 to 202. The minimum age for marriage was raised to 15 for women and 18 for men (Art 144), and the requirement of the parents' authorisation was made much stiffer. Women under 21 and men under 25 required the agreement of both parents, or in case of disagreement, authorisation by the father. Above those ages the parents' consent was not legally necessary, but 'children of the family' must formally solicit their advice on three occasions (by *acte respectueux*), a single solicitation sufficing in the case of daughters aged 25 and sons aged 30. These formalities, required in deference to the 'cult of filial piety', would serve to delay the marriage.

The marriage ceremony takes place in the town hall before a state official and four witnesses (Art 75), two oral pronouncements being required (one only was required in 1792). Fewer grounds of opposition to a marriage were allowed than under the old law, but proceedings to have a marriage annulled on the grounds 'of public order and morality' could be brought by 'anyone with an interest' or by the state representative (Art 184). In this respect marriage is a 'public treaty' (Gillet), subject to state supervision. As to avoidance for mistake there was considerable debate. Bonaparte thought that the choice of the parties should be free based on their feelings, but the codifiers retained the traditional restrictive view and the Code mentions only error *in persona* (Art 180). The different grounds of annulment have different rules, but nullity could often be cured by subsequent events (Arts 181 and 185) so the number of cases was kept down.

B. Marriage – an unequal partnership

Being designed for the perpetuation of the human race, marriage gives rise to an obligation on the part of the spouses to 'feed, maintain and bring up their children' (Art 203). This alimentary obligation is reciprocal. A child, however, has no right to a dowry, since such a demand might threaten 'domestic governance' (Portalis).

The spouses' duty of 'mutual fidelity, assistance and consortium' (Art 212) is likewise reciprocal, but since conjugal partnership cannot exist 'unless one of the spouses is subordinated to the other' the following articles emphasise the 'dominance of the husband'. Art 213, which was not in the committee's draft, provides that '[T]he husband must protect the wife, the wife obey the husband'. The independence which women had claimed during the Revolution had clearly gone. The wife can have no domicile other than that of her husband and cannot bring a lawsuit without her husband's authorisation, and although a woman who is a 'public merchant' may enter obligations 'arising out of her business' a wife is otherwise incapable of acquiring or disposing of property 'unless her husband joins in the transfer or consents in writing'. The requisite authorisation may be supplied by the court if the husband refuses it or is convicted or interdicted, missing or under age. Lack of authorisation can be adduced by the woman as well as the man or his heirs (Art 225), which suggests that she is treated as incapable not merely out of respect for the husband but also because of the inexperience of the weaker sex.

C. Divorce – the 'ultimate recourse'

The provisions regarding divorce in the Code are the outcome of rather a diffuse discussion – for Portalis divorce was acceptable only because it left the churches free to decide on the matter, Maleville and Tronchet were disinclined to accept it, and opinion in the *Conseil d'État* was divided, though it finally voted to maintain it. Bonaparte played an important part in the discussion by stressing the usefulness of divorce as a solution to divisions within families.

As in the committee's draft, the principal ground for divorce was fault, especially adultery. Here there was a striking inequality between man and wife: the husband could always invoke his wife's adultery as a ground of divorce (Art 229), but she could do so only 'if he kept his mistress in the family home'. The adulterous wife was also subject to a criminal sanction under the *Code civil*: she could be condemned to reside in a place of correction for at least three months and possibly for two years (Art 298).

Other grounds of divorce were abuse, violence and grossly insulting behaviour; either party could rely on these but it was for the judge to decide. In all cases proceedings took place in court, when the judge could make 'observations', urge reconciliation and possibly call witnesses to give oral testimony. Judgment was given in open court. Divorce was accordingly something quite different from the 'family gatherings' system under the Revolution: it was a solemn and expensive drama. The dignity of marriage was further enhanced by providing that divorced persons could not remarry each other (Art 295), and that the adulterer could not marry his lover. Custody of children was in principle accorded to the successful claimant for divorce, though the court might decide otherwise in exceptional cases in the 'greater interests of the children' (Art 302).

Incompatibility of temperament had been an accepted ground of divorce in 1792, but it was allowed under the Code only if the parties were agreed that 'life together was insupportable' and proved that there was a 'manifest reason for the divorce'. It is not clear whether in allowing divorce on this ground the legislator was really admitting that mutual incompatibility sufficed by itself or was simply providing a way of concealing misconduct which was the true cause of the rupture. Couples were deterred from resorting lightly to this ground of divorce, for it was attended by many tiresome restrictions and consequences. The husband must be over 25 and the wife over 21 but less than 45, and the marriage must have lasted at least two years and not more than twenty. In order to avoid public scandal the procedure was more private, and subject to family control: the spouses needed the express authorisation of their parents, as if they were still minors (Art 278). Finally, life for parties divorced by mutual consent was made quite difficult: they had to appear before the judge on several occasions during the following year, they could not remarry for three years, and they must, in favour of their children, waive their right to half of their property. The *Code civil* did its very best to see that divorce would not, as some people thought, be too frequently sought on this ground.

The canonical institution of *divortium a mensa et thoro* had been abolished during the Revolution, but owing to Maleville and Tronchet judicial separation was brought back into the Code, and could be sought whenever there were grounds for divorce. It had the effect that the marriage link survived and so prevented remarriage. Such separation involved a separation of the property, but the wife's incapacity was not wholly removed, since she could not by herself dispose of landed property (Art 1449).

II. Establishing parenthood

Given their aim of 'perpetuating families and keeping them distinct' the codifiers were determined that there should be clear rules for establishing parenthood, especially paternity, as indicated by the rubric of Title VII of Book One. Despite references to science (Fourcroy was consulted on the period of gestation) something more was required than recourse to nature, the fact of paternity being 'covered by an impenetrable veil'. The law had been thrown into confusion by revolutionary texts (Law of 2 November 1793 – 12 *brumaire* II – on the rights of children born outside marriage) and radical drafts (as on adoption), so the codifiers sought to restore the situation by making the law 'more severe and restrictive' (Lahary) as regards children, whether legitimate (A), natural (B), or adopted (C).

A. Legitimacy and 'families at peace'

The legitimacy of the children of a marriage was to be clearly established, as far as possible free from doubt and 'unusual circumstances'. First of all, the *Code civil* reinforces the presumption of paternity – *pater est is quem nuptiae demonstrant* – a rule whose origin is lost 'in the night of time', according to Bigot de Préameneu. If a child is conceived during marriage the husband is taken to be his father, provided conception took place between 300 and 180 days prior to the birth, the legal period (Art 312). To this rule, stoutly defended by Bonaparte, there were very few exceptions: it applied unless sexual congress between husband and wife had been impossible (due to absence or accident, but not to alleged impotence), or the wife had committed adultery and concealed the birth (Art 313). The husband could refuse to acknowledge a child born less than 180 days after the wedding except in a few situations: if he knew of the pregnancy before the wedding, if he participated in the birth certificate, or if the child was still-born (Art 314). In any case he must act within one or two months (Art 316), and immediately 'exclude from the family' a child he regards as no part of it. Only if he dies within the period when he himself could have brought the claim can his heirs act in his place.

The legitimacy of children is in general proved by the birth certificate (Art 319). Should the register be lost or destroyed, legitimate children are allowed to rely on factual evidence, such as having the father's name (*nomen*), having been treated by the father as his child (*tractatus*) or recognised by the family or neighbours (*fama*) – Arts 320 and 321. The legitimacy of a child who has a birth certificate and corresponding factual status is beyond cavil. Failing this, a child can establish its legitimacy in court by witnesses, provided there is a document on which proof can be built, or extremely cogent evidence (Art 323). Time does not run against the child on this point: 'it is not a question of mere property, since civil status affects the person as well' (Bigot de Préameneu).

B. The illegitimate child and social order

The codifiers quite realised that children born outside marriage are 'innocent victims of the fault of their parents', but in order to preserve the family and maintain social order they nevertheless drew a line between those who were legitimate and those who were not (for example Art 338). It is not enough for the latter to produce a birth certificate or establish factual status; voluntary recognition is required, either in the birth certificate or by notarial act, and even this is not possible if the child is the product of incest or adultery ('morally deplorable'). Otherwise recognition is possible by either father or mother independently: recognition by the father, unless contested by the mother, is valid but has effect only as regards himself (Art 336). In providing that one can be the child of one parent and not the other the Code has come a long way from the revolutionary view of marriage as a mere informal arrangement between the parents.

It is nearly impossible for the illegitimate child to sue his father. Art 340 provides that 'inquiry into paternity is forbidden', a trenchant formula designed to put an end to the abusive allegations of paternity such as were rife in the *ancien régime* and which Bigot de Préameneu called 'the scourge of society'. The only exception to this prohibition, owing to the insistence of Cambacérès and the intervention of the Tribunate, is where the mother had been kidnapped at the time of conception. Even here the courts have the option of refusing to declare the paternity of the ravisher: the desire to restrain the 'perversity of branded and shameless women' could trump the need to protect the inexperienced from the 'dangers of seduction'. Since in the absence of marriage the law 'knows only the mother', maternity may be the subject of inquiry provided some document can serve as a basis of proof (Art 341). Children born of incest or adultery cannot seek a declaration of either paternity or maternity: they are regarded as 'monsters whose very existence should be forgotten'.

Involuntary recognition having been reduced to the minimum and voluntary recognition being discouraged – as Bonaparte said, 'society has no interest in the recognition of bastards' – the chapter on illegitimate children starts out with legitimation, as the sole means of putting an end to 'disorder'. Subsequent marriage of the parents can 'elevate' children born previously, provided that recognition took place before the marriage or is noted in the marriage certificate (Art 331). Once again, children of adultery and incest were excluded.

C. Adoption – a study in legislation

Adoption had been recognised under the Revolution, though no precise rules were laid down for it, but the decision to include it in the *Code civil* was only taken after heated discussion in the *Conseil d'État*. The codifiers and even Bonaparte himself hesitated for some time between the alternatives of regarding adoption as a public reward for civic service, granted by the highest authorities of the state, and of treating it as a private matter designed to allow owners of property, especially businessmen and industrialists, to choose who should succeed to their name and property. The choice of a 'personal contract' finally won through, as it had done in the Prussian Code.

Adoption was at first thought of as a kind of consolation prize in the interests of the person effecting the adoption, who could be a person of either sex, married or not (with the consent of the spouse, if married), but must be at least 50 years old (lest people choose to avoid getting married) and without legitimate descendants at the time of the adoption (Art 343). Prior to the adoption the 'parent' must have cared for the child for a continuous period of at least six years during his minority, a precondition which was waived where the younger party had heroically saved the life of the adopter by 'rescuing him from affray, fire or flood'. The 'contract' of adoption could not be finalised until the person adopted reached majority. Nor need the child be an orphan or abandoned, for until he was 25 the consent of any surviving parent or the advice of a parental council was required.

Adoption was essentially a court matter. After the agreement between the parties had been formalised before the *juge de paix*, the tribunal of first instance checked that the legal conditions were satisfied and that the party making the adoption was 'of good reputation'. The tribunal then decided, without giving reasons, to allow or prohibit the adoption, a judgment which the court of appeal had to confirm or vacate. Once the adoption was approved it was made public and entered in the register of civil status.

One of the main consequences of adoption was that the person adopted added the name of his adoptive parent to his own. The fact of having two names showed that there had been no change of family: the person adopted stayed in his natural family and retained his rights as such, including rights of inheritance (Art 348). The 'quasi-paternity resulting from the adoption' (Berlier) furthermore gave the adopted person the same rights of succession as a legitimate child of the quasi-parent, without creating any link between him and the adopter's family. Adoption could be preceded by 'informal guardianship' (*tutelle officieuse*), a legal relationship (endorsed by the judge), between any person at least 50 years old and a person less than 15, provided the spouse of the former and the parents of the latter gave their consent. The guardian was bound to feed the pupil and fit him for gainful employment, and could adopt him by will after five years or on his majority; indeed, if he failed to do so on request, he was liable if the pupil had no means of earning his living. This 'new way of helping children' (Gary) seems designed to supplement the institution of adoption which had been reduced to the minimum.

III. Keeping the family in order

In the discussions leading up to the Code the family was often referred to as a 'special and distinctive partnership', which needed a leader (A) so as 'to keep it in order' (Réal). Though parents might be 'the best defenders of their children' (Leroy), the state might still have to intervene in order to forestall disorder, so rules were introduced to protect weaker parties such as minor children under guardianship (B), interdicted persons and spendthrifts (C).

A. The father as judge

The codifiers were keen to reinstate paternal power, which had been brought into question under the Revolution. The rubric of Title IX of Book One is accordingly 'Of paternal power', although the term 'authority' was also used (Art 372) and the 'voice of nature' was mentioned in speeches. Thus the very first article in the title (Art 371) reads: 'Children of all ages must honour and respect their father and mother', a text which, according to Bigot de Préameneu, contains 'principles which the following articles merely develop by spelling out their consequences'.

Paternal power, often called '*magistrature*' (magistracy), inhered in the father personally. The father alone had authority over minor children during the marriage (Art 373), and his power of correction is much greater than that accorded to the widowed mother (provided she has not remarried), who puts in an appearance only eight articles later. Recognised illegitimate children are subject to parental control like legitimate children (Art 383). Grand-parents are not mentioned at all, for, as Tronchet said, 'the son belongs exclusively to the father'.

Paternal power, the power to give orders and lay down rules, is not defined by the *Code civil*, nor is its function clearly identified, except possibly through Arts 203 and 385 which state that parents are to feed, maintain and bring up their children 'in accordance with their means'. Although Bonaparte wanted to include education, drawing a distinction between sons and daughters, and giving some authority to the mother as 'natural instructress of the children', the *Code civil* vests all the power in the father. The father's authorisation is required if the child wants to leave home, unless he is 18 and proposes to enlist. The father can even have his child locked up 'if his conduct is really intolerable;' the father can demand a judicial arrest warrant for up to a month until the child is 16, and thereafter, until his majority; and the president of the local court may grant an order of detention for not more than six months (Arts 376 and 377). The revolutionary 'family tribunal' no longer existed as such, so the proceedings were judicial, but neither public nor confrontational, since 'children's misconduct was a family matter' (Vesin). No formality or writing apart from the order for arrest was required, and the father could forgive the child and shorten the period of detention. The child's only recourse was to write to the appeal court to have the dossier re-examined in secret. Some protection was afforded when the child had property or an occupation of its own, or the father had remarried: the widow required the consent of two close relatives of the deceased father.

Parental power also comprised some 'economic rights' vested in the father, or the widowed mother: until he reached the age of 18 or earlier emancipation (Art 384) they could use his property, apart from assets he had acquired by working or had been left or given to him for his own use. The codifiers retained from revolutionary law the rule that on reaching the age of 21 a child became emancipated (Art 388 – the sole article in the chapter on 'Minority'); by so doing they hoped to prevent the 'paternal despotism' which had existed under the old order.

B. Guardianship and emancipation

The rules regarding guardianship are drawn from several different sources of earlier law. Despite references to 'the interests of the child', especially as regards emancipation, the emphasis was on 'protecting rights of property' (Leroy). Thus the chapter on 'Guardianship' starts out by providing that during the marriage the property of minor children is to be administered by the father (Art 389); after his death guardianship vests in the mother. If the father has reservations about his wife's abilities he may nominate a council whose agreement is necessary for the exercise of her guardianship (Art 391). We can therefore infer that when the codifiers said that they wanted to avoid 'undue inequality between the sexes' (Berlier) there were some inequalities which they found quite acceptable. Should the widow remarry she may continue as guardian only if a family council summoned by herself so decides.

A child orphaned during minority may have a guardian appointed by the will of the last of his parents to die, but in the absence of any such provision, one of his ascendants, preferably on his father's side, is chosen as statutory guardian. If testamentary guardianship shows the law's trust in the parents, statutory guardianship is regarded as 'a necessary consequence of the very organisation of the family' (Leroy). In the absence of ascendants, and subject to the dispensations contained in Arts 427–449, the guardian (who must be male) is chosen by a family council consisting of six relatives or in-laws presided over by the local judge. The fact that three of the six relatives are chosen from each side shows the codifiers' preference for relationships by blood, and their desire to prevent manipulation is inferable from preference being given to closeness of relationship and seniority; mere friends of the family are involved only as a last resort.

The guardian is bound to look after the person and property of the minor 'like a good father,' but even when the guardianship is vested in a parent, the agreement of the family council (a sort of domestic court), and sometimes that of a judge, is required for really important decisions, such as whether to accept an inheritance or gift, to borrow money, or to dispose of or charge landed property. This strict regulation is designed to protect the child's immovable property, for his movable property is generally sold so that the income exceeds the outgoings.

When the child is 15 he may be emancipated by his father, failing whom, the mother; if neither is alive, he must wait until 18 and requires a decision of the family council. The emancipated minor enjoys personal freedom but is capable of 'merely administrative' acts (Art 481) – unless he is in business, when he is 'deemed to be an adult as regards business dealings' (Art 487). Certain transactions, however, such as selling or burdening real property, still require the agreement of a curator or even the permission of the family council. The emancipated child is seen as being groomed for adulthood under the supervision of the courts, which can reduce obligations which are unduly burdensome and even revoke the emancipation.

C. *Incapable adults*

The *Code civil* permits the interdiction of adults who are 'imbecile, demented or uncontrollable'. The imbecile and demented can be interdicted only on the proposal of a relative, the preservation of his property being purely a family matter, but in cases of 'uncontrolled rage' a state official may act if the relatives fail to do so. The decision on interdiction or the need to have a council involved in certain transactions is made by the court after ascertaining the views of the family council and examining the person involved. Once interdicted the person is given a guardian and treated much as a minor. The wife may act as her husband's guardian, but since – according to Bertrand de Greuille – women are naive, she is subject to control by the family council. In order to prevent the person under interdict being exploited by his family, most of his income must be devoted to 'making his life easier and facilitating his recovery' (Art 510).

As to spendthrifts, the codifiers decided after much hesitation that they could be enjoined from litigating, borrowing or disposing of property without the consent of a council appointed by the court. The state was justified in intervening by its interest in the 'preservation of families', whose fortunes could be ruined by the spendthrift's feckless dealings with his property, the spendthrift being, according to Emmery, 'a kind of madman'.

Section 3: Economic relations in the family

The links between family and property in the *Code civil* are numerous. Even civil status and parental relationship could be presented by the codifiers as forms of property, and the rules on matrimonial property regimes (I) and inheritance (II), for all that they are placed in Book Three of the Code on 'the different methods of acquiring property', are only the counterpart in property law of the relations laid down in Book One on husband and wife and on parents and children.

I. The range of property régimes

Under the old order there had been a plethora of matrimonial property regimes and as they had not been directly altered under the Revolution the codifiers merely made some 'adjustments' so as not to disrupt popular practices in this area. Art 1387 provides that parties are free to choose their preferred regime, subject only to a certain number of mandatory rules of *ordre public*. The terms of the chosen regime cannot detract from the rights of the husband as 'head of the family' (Art 1388), nor alter the statutory order of succession (Art 1389). Nor can reference be made to any rule of customary law or pre-Codal legislation: the survival of practices under the *ancien régime* was acceptable, but not resort to obsolete law. Marriage contracts must be drawn up before a notary prior to the wedding and could not be altered thereafter. In the absence of a contract, the regime of community of assets, the 'common law of France', applied, and it was to this regime that the codifiers, after much discussion, gave priority (A). An important place was, however, left for the dowry or dotal system (B), and other models were on offer so as to widen the range of choice (C).

A. Community property

In treating the community of movables and acquisitions as the regime 'most favourable to social order' and 'most concordant with the national character' (Berlier) the codifiers were following customary law. This default regime also seemed best adapted to 'relatively poor families' and to 'countrymen and artisans' (Duveyrier). Since the spouses might have owned landed property prior to marriage (then called 'their own property') or obtained it during the marriage by inheritance or gift the code proceeds to identify what is comprised in the community and what is deductible from it (Arts 1401–1420).

As 'head of the community and in charge of its acquisitions' the husband has sole management of community property. He can sell or charge common property by himself (Arts 1421), but his power to make gifts is subject to a 'reasonable restriction' – under Arts 1422 and 1423 he may not give away landed property held in common, nor all or any fraction of the movables save for the 'establishment of children of the marriage', and he cannot by will dispose of more than his half of the community property. The married woman's incapacity is reinforced: she cannot bind the community without the consent of her husband (unless she is a 'public merchant') and her personal property is administered by the husband, though he cannot alienate it without her consent.

When the community is dissolved, the wife becomes once again an 'associée', as under customary law. She may accept or decline the community (Art 1453). In the latter case she can claim only her own immovable property or what it fetched, from the personal property of her husband if the community assets are inadequate. If she accepts, adjustments are made if the personal property of the spouses has been alienated or improved at the cost of the community, and she is protected to the extent that her liability for community debts is limited to the amount she obtains from it.

B. The dowry system

A chapter of more than 40 articles is devoted to the dowry system. Although its origins are Roman, it is not special to any particular part of France but is available to any couple that prefers it. The characteristic of the regime is not the fact that the bride brings a dowry with her (for there may well be dowry under a community regime) but in the way the law treats the dowry and any other property the wife may have.

The dowry, usually provided by the bride's relatives, may consist of some or all of the woman's present and future property, or even of a specific object, depending on the terms of the marriage contract. It is administered by the husband during the subsistence of the marriage (Art 1549), but he cannot mortgage landed property (Art 1554) which may, however, be sold if the marriage contract so provides (Art 1557), or in order to provide for the children, and in certain cases by court order (for example, in order to obtain the release of either party from prison or to make an advantageous exchange). On the legal position of movables the *Code civil* is silent, even when addressing the incapacities of the married woman, but the regime is obviously set up in order to 'protect the wife from her own weakness' (Berlier) and to keep the property within the family. On the death of the husband the dowry falls to the widow, on the death of the wife to her heirs; to ensure this, the property is subject to a legal charge subject only to the rights of creditors prior to the marriage.

The woman may have property not included in the dowry. This is called 'paraphernal'. The wife can administer and enjoy such property, but cannot dispose of it without the consent of her husband (Art 1576), contrary to the position under the *ancien régime*, and she is encouraged by Arts 1577 and 1578 to grant the power of administration to her husband. It was no part of the codifiers' aim to give the woman any real independence: that 'would be contrary to her interest, a denial of nature and inconsistent with the law of France' (Duveyrier).

C. A menu of optional clauses

After the chapter devoted to the statutory community regime the *Code civil* sets out in Arts 1497–1539 quite a long but not restrictive list of terms which parties can include in their marriage contract so as to modify the statutory regime or create a regime of their own. These optional clauses can limit the community to assets acquired during the marriage, or provide for the inclusion of identified landed property within the community (this is called '*ameublissement*'), or create a community of all the property of the parties.

There are even clauses on offer (though the codifiers did not expect them to be used very often) which exclude community property altogether yet fall short of the dowry system. In such a regime the husband administers all the wife's property, whose income is to 'meet the expenses of the marriage' (Art 1530), unless there is a clause giving the wife an annuity 'for her maintenance and personal requirements'. The wife's property is to be restored when the marriage ends, but is not inalienable. If the contract provides for *separate property* 'the wife retains full administrative control of her property, movable and immovable' and makes a contribution to the expenses of the marriage, usually one-third of the expenses unless otherwise agreed. The wife cannot, however, dispose of landed property without the specific authorisation of her husband or the court (Art 1538), which reminds us that the 'law of the marriage', namely the wife's subjection to the husband, remains in force as long as the marriage itself.

II. The 'liberal' law of inheritance

The codifiers were at one in regarding succession as a matter for the state. As Siméon said '(O)n our death any connection we had with our property is broken; only the law can renew it'. Tronchet held likewise that it was not by natural law that relatives inherit the property of the deceased, but by state law, which also prescribed the order of succession (A). On this view, the power to dispose of property by will is a concession granted to fathers, one which relieves the state of 'some of its concern' (Portalis) (B).

A. Order of succession, closeness of relationship

If the decedent has left no will, 'the law determines the order of succession' (Art 723) and, contrary to the rules under many of the customs, does this regardless of the nature of the property or its source (Art 732). The *Code civil* puts the children of the decedent and their issue at the head of the list of 'legitimate heirs', and then his ascendants and collaterals (Art 731). In so doing the law claims to be respecting the decedent's 'natural and legitimate affections', his 'presumed will' (Treilhard), as well as recognising the rights of the members of his family.

Legitimate children are all treated equally: the law draws no distinction according to their gender or seniority or whether they are the children of a first or later marriage. The part of any child already dead passes without limit of degree to his descendants – a 'legal fiction' (Art 739). In the absence of descendants, ascendants and collaterals succeed. Here a 'split' occurs (*la fente* occurred in many customs and was accepted by revolutionary law), severing the estate into two equal parts, one for the paternal and one for the maternal line. Half of the estate is split between the surviving parents, while brothers and sisters ('privileged' collaterals, as are their descendants) succeed to the other half (or three-quarters if either the father or mother has died). Thereafter other ascendants take (the closest in each line being preferred, with collaterals taking if an ascendant in that line fails), and finally collaterals to the twelfth degree, beyond which it is assumed that the family link has faded away. Here again the rule of *la fente* applies, but in the absence of a qualified heir in one line the property goes to the other (Art 755). Quite apart from this, ascendants may reclaim anything they gave to their childless descendants (Art 747).

The *Code civil* then turns to 'irregular successions' where there is no legitimate heir 'within the family', a phrase used to exclude natural children. Only if a natural child has been recognised does he still have the rights of a blood relation, though he is 'not within the family' (Siméon), and the law allows him a right to succeed 'proportional to the value of the property' – reduced if there are legitimate children (one-third of the part of a legitimate child, Art 757) and increased if there are only ascendants or privileged collaterals (one-half of their portion) or more distant collaterals (three-quarters). Furthermore, if the parents during their lifetime give the illegitimate child half of what he would obtain on their death, he has no further claim (Art 761), which protects the family from any claim by such an 'odious creditor', as Siméon called him. In addition, according to Art 337, in the title on parentage, the natural child who has been recognised by only one of the parents has no rights if their marriage produced offspring. The 'miserable fruit' of adulterous or incestuous congress, supposing that there is some indirect proof of actual parentage, obtain nothing but a payment for support, and that by way of 'charity'.

The surviving spouse is also considered an irregular successor, but is even less favoured than the illegitimate child, for the spouse takes in preference only to the state. 'The surviving spouse, however closely linked to the decedent, belongs to a different family.' (Siméon). Finally, the state receives estates where there is no individual successor, for 'what belongs to no individual belongs to the body social'. Whereas legitimate heirs find vested in them automatically 'the property, rights and claims of the decedent' (Art 724), those who succeed irregularly must go to court for an order sending them into possession of the estate. Legitimate heirs are free to reject the succession, or to accept it, with or without benefit of inventory. Joint heirs are always entitled to demand the division of the landed or immovable property so as to take their separate part (Art 826), notwithstanding the law's distaste for the 'division of estates and the splitting of enterprises'.

B. Freedom and family obligations

When Bigot de Préameneu proposed the title of the *Code civil* on donations and wills he used the terms 'freedom of disposition and family obligations'. The question was what part of his estate a decedent should be free to dispose of. The revolutionary law of 6 January 1794 (17 *nivôse* year II) had allowed free disposition of only a very small part of the estate, but those who prepared the draft of 1801 and the members of the legislative section of the *Conseil d'État* wanted to adopt the innovation in the Law of 25 March 1800 (4 *germinal* year VIII) which fixed it at a quarter of the property of the decedent with any descendants. The heated discussion in the *Conseil d'État* in the opening months of 1803 makes it clear that the question raised in the *Constituante* of equality in succession rights remained a burning issue. Maleville, Tronchet and Portalis wanted to increase the father's power 'to reward and punish;' Bonaparte was concerned with the 'undue subdivision' of modest fortunes; and Berlier and Réal were afraid of any return to primogeniture.

The compromise was found by Cambacérès: the reserved portion was to depend on the number of children. If there was one legitimate child, gifts could not exceed half of the property, a third if there were two, and a quarter if three or more (Art 913). If there were only ascendants a half or three-quarters could be disposed of. By contrast collaterals had no entitlement: owners were not to be deprived of 'the full freedom to help enterprise to develop in the face of all its risks'. The testator could give or bequeath his disposable portion to any of his legitimate children without their being required to account for it (Art 919). To this extent he could show his affection for a particular child or admiration for his industry. Such gifts could not, however, put illegitimate children in any better position (Art 908). The testator could not require an heir to transfer the property to anyone else: such 'substitutions' were prohibited by the Code, for they could 'sacrifice' all the other members of a family 'in order to give one of them a brilliant fortune'. They could, however, leave property to a child, perhaps suspected of being light-headed, on the condition that he pass it on to his own children equally (Art 1048): this was to 'preserve the power of parents to act justly'. Donations to a spouse, which were inherently revocable by the donor, could not, if there were issue, exceed a quarter absolutely plus a life interest in a further quarter (Art 1094), and a gift to a second spouse, if the previous marriage had issue, could not exceed the amount to which fell to the least favoured of the legitimate children.

Permitted donations could be made *inter vivos* in front of a notary (Art 931) and rendered irrevocable except for failure of condition, birth of subsequent children or ingratitude on the part of the donee, as specified by law. Alternatively, they could be made by will. Following Daguesseau's ordinance of 1735, three forms of will were possible; the holographic will (handwritten by the testator), the public will (made in front of two notaries in the presence of two witnesses) and the mystic will (written or dictated by the testator, and presented closed and sealed to a notary with at least six witnesses). There were special rules for soldiers, sailors and French persons abroad. All of these wills could include specific bequests, bequests of a specified part of the estate, or residuary legacies (*legs particulier, legs universel, legs à titre universel*). The residuary legatee took automatically only if there were no legitimate heirs (Art 1006).

The *Code civil* also had a special chapter on distributions by ascendants. They could in their lifetime divide up their property among their issue, especially in order to 'avoid dismemberment' and to leave one of the children in the family home. As this 'could greatly affect the fate of the family' (Bigot de Préameneu), such a division must be consistent with the rules as to the reserved portion and could be attacked by an heir who received less than three-quarters of his entitlement (Art 1079). The codifiers thought that this institution would prove 'very beneficial' in 'establishing order in the family' (Jaubert), and Sédillez called it 'the finest title in the *Code civil*', as regulating 'the effects of liberality' and reinforcing the power of the father.

Chapter 3: Law for Property Owners

Books Two and Three of the *Code civil*, containing Arts 1766 through 2281, are devoted to ownership and its modifications, and the different ways of acquiring it. This by itself is enough to show that ownership is the centrepiece of the *Code Napoléon*, as the draftsmen readily admitted. For Portalis ownership is 'the immanent spirit of the legislation' and Grenier observed that to a certain extent the *Code civil* is concerned throughout with the exercise of property rights (persons and family being the other fundamental axis of the Code, as we have seen). The Code accordingly draws no great distinction between property and obligations: if Book Two of the Code seeks to define and circumscribe the rights in property (Section 1), contracts, extra-contractual obligations and securities are treated in Book Three as methods of transferring, exploiting and guaranteeing them (Section 2).

Section 1: Ownership defined and limited

Art 544, so characteristic of the private law of its day, is often taken to symbolise the whole of Book Two of the *Code civil*, with the rest of the Book, narrower in scope and more technically drafted, relegated to the background. The contrast should not be exaggerated, however, since Art 544 must be read in the context of other articles of the Code, but it does illustrate the tension between treating ownership as unitary in the spirit of the declarations during the Revolution (I) and having a law of property with 'modifications', reminiscent of prior law (II).

I. A revolutionary definition

The very fact that, unlike Roman or earlier law, the *Code civil* defines ownership suggests that it conceives of 'the right of ownership' as monolithic and individuated. This is in line with the Revolutionary Declarations of Human Rights: that of 1789 made ownership 'a right sacred and inviolable' – as did those of 1793 and 1795, which defined it. Those declarations are the source of 'the right to enjoy and dispose' of property (A) whereas the pleonastic addition of 'in the most absolute manner' (B) and the qualification regarding laws and regulations (C) rather reflect the concerns of the codifiers under the Consulate.

A. The right of enjoyment and disposition

The definition of ownership in Art 544 as the 'right to enjoy and dispose of things' asserts some ideas and suggests others. Ownership is presented as a right exercisable by man (even if the Tribune Grenier saw in it 'a moral quality inherent in things'), though the Code does not say who can exercise this right, whereas the Declaration of the Rights of Man and the Citizen of 24 June 1793 proclaimed that the right inhered in 'every citizen'. The two fundamental prerogatives of the owner are mentioned: the right to enjoy, corresponding to the *usus* and *fructus* of the Romanists from Bartolus to Pothier, and the right of disposal, conferred on 'individuals' by Art 537, so freeing the circulation of property from the obstacles which existed under prior law. The 'things' to which the right of enjoyment and disposal attaches remain unspecified, but surely must include assets of all types: there is no mention of income, the product of work and industry, as there was in the declarations of rights of 1793 and 1795.

If this definition of ownership is extremely laconic the theoretical discussion in the *travaux préparatoires* was extensive. Portalis in particular saw ownership as a right whose principle inhered 'in the very constitution of our being'. It was originally natural, first applied to chattels when captured or made, and then extended to land, but even so 'it was not in natural law that one must look for the rules relating to it'. Chabot de l'Allier and other draftsmen of the *Code civil* were of the view that 'society is the sole and true source of ownership'. Art 544 does nothing to resolve the controversy whether ownership is natural or social in origin.

B. 'In the most absolute manner'

This somewhat superfluous phrase is probably due to the legislative section of the *Conseil d'État*, for the draft of the government committee preferred to speak of 'full ownership'. Insistence on the absolute right of disposition certainly serves to distinguish ownership from usufruct, but the principal purpose of the change was to prevent any return to feudalism or the concept of 'divided estates' characteristic of a system of tenures. Several articles of the Code show that people at the time were afraid of the resurrection of real burdens, with their hint of feudalism. For example, Art 530 provides that all real burdens are 'essentially commutable', as under the Revolution, Art 686 makes it impossible to create a servitude which imposes any obligation to provide services, and the provisions on leases of 'rural properties' are designed to prevent the use of the device of tacit relocation to create a perpetual right of enjoyment in the lessee (Art 1755). Ownership is thus not only freed from 'these feudal features, gone forever' (Treilhard) but also from communal restraints: the owner is free to enclose his property and thereby put a stop to public grazing (Arts 647–648).

Finally, the word 'absolute', which Mirabeau had used in 1789 when speaking of the individual as 'absolute master' of his property, would reassure the owners who had purchased confiscated property and were worried by the 'false theories' of ownership against which Portalis and Grenier inveighed. It was not, however, the aim of the codifiers to make the owner 'sovereign' with unlimited rights over the property: as Grenier said, '[I]t is revolting to think that there could be any right to abuse the right of ownership.'

C. Limits imposed by laws and regulations

Portalis distinguished between the freedom to be enjoyed by the owner and the licence which complete independence would permit. Art 544 thus puts a limit to the rights of the owner by prohibiting 'use contrary to law or regulation', the latter relating to the enhanced power to make regulations under the Constitution of 1799 and the practice of the administration (still called 'police regulations'). Art 545 proceeds to state that private ownership must yield to 'public utility', though such expropriation 'called for a just indemnity, payable in advance'. This might seem to be treating the state as if it were just an individual buying property from another, but the codifiers were in no doubt that private ownership was subject to 'the great idea of the public good'.

Public property is regulated in Arts 537–541, but private property is by no means unregulated. As we have seen, the freedom of spendthrifts of full age to dispose of their property was subject to serious limitation, and owners could not make dispositions which would reduce the rights of legitimate heirs. In Book Two, the rights of owners may be affected by legislation and regulations relating to mining (Art 552), and 'special laws control the use of woods and forests' (Art 636) as well as the 'freedom to hunt and fish' (Art 715). Finally, for Portalis, 'it should not be open to an owner to thwart the general plans of the public administration by building on his property as he chooses'.

Because man must respect the rights of his fellow humans – there are, as Portalis said, 'obligations and services which an owner owes to his links with the community and cannot justly ignore' – the *Code civil* provides for 'servitudes' or '*services fonciers*'. Some of these derive from the location of the properties: for example, properties downhill are bound to receive water from properties above them (Art 640), and if the property has a spring, the owner may use the water from it as he likes (Art 641), but he may not change the course of its flow if it provides water for a village (Art 643). Likewise in balancing the rights of the individual and the public good a person with riparian property may use the water from the river for irrigation, but if conflicts arise it is for the courts to resolve them by 'reconciling agricultural needs with the respect due to ownership'. Other 'legal' servitudes include party walls and ditches as well as the right of way to an enclave, that is property with no other access. Where the servitude is 'of use to individuals' only the owner of the neighbouring property can invoke this restriction on the servient owner's rights (Arts 649 and 651).

II. A more traditional view

Most of the detailed rules regarding rights of property, though not inconsistent with the new view of ownership, are not really innovations by the codifiers, who took their solutions as regards the different kinds of property from customary law (A) and its 'modalities' from Roman Law and doctrine (B).

A. The different kinds of property

Book Two of the *Code civil* starts out with a trope from customary law: 'All property is either movable or immovable.' Pothier is the main source of the subdivision of immovables into those which are immovable by nature (land and buildings), immovables by destination (things put on the land for its use and things permanently attached to it) and assets rendered immovable by their function as regards the land (rights and claims regarding an immovable). The list of things which are immovables by destination includes both items of traditional agronomy (cattle, ploughing instruments, pigeons in dovecotes, rabbits in a warren and hives for the honey-bee) and those of nascent industry (forges, paper works and other 'factories'). The idea is that an estate constitutes a unit and that it is an 'encouragement to farming' to treat as immovables the objects which subserve that aim (the word 'exploitation' is used in Art 524).

When rents and offices ceased to be incorporeal immovables as they were under prior law, movable property, as the codifiers explicitly said, was to become a more important part of the citizen's wealth, now including not only cattle, boats and *meubles meublants* (furniture in apartments, Art 534) but also cash, credits, obligations and claims such as annuities. Shares in 'companies engaged in finance, commerce and industry' were treated as movables because 'what they produce is movable' (Treilhard) and because the immovable property in such enterprises is owned by a 'legal person' (Goupil-Préfeln). Rents are in law movables and 'purely personal assets' because they can exist independently of any mortgage on the land, so it was quite logical of the *Code civil* to accept by analogy that incorporeal assets could be owned, and even possessed (Art 2228).

The aim was not to rank the different classes of items of property as regards their value but simply to distinguish them 'in the manner most advantageous to the owner' (Savoye-Rollin). The distinction between movables and immovables was no longer as important in the law of succession as it had been before the Revolution, but it remained significant in matrimonial property regimes, in the law of securities and as to prescription. For immovables the codifiers adopted the long periods of prescription of Roman law (10, 20 or 30 years: Arts 2262–2265); but it was from the case law of the Châtelet of Paris that they took the principle that 'as to movables, possession equals title' (Art 2279), recognising that movables are transferred by simple delivery, passing as they do from hand to hand.

B. *Modalities of ownership*

The *Code civil* has more than thirty articles on the law of 'accession', the different ways in which one thing can be produced from, or joined to, or incorporated in, another. While leaving a certain latitude to the courts and allowing recourse to 'natural equity' (Art 565) the codifiers were ready to adopt doctrines of Roman law such as *specificatio* (when a person uses someone else's property to make a thing of a different kind, Art 570). They all rest on the idea that 'everything which is united with or absorbed in another thing belongs to the owner of the latter', eschewing economic considerations in favour of the 'owner of a thing already in existence' (Grenier). Ownership of land is accordingly extended as far as possible, above and below the surface, to earth washed on to it and to islands formed in non-navigable rivers, with a provision that when a river leaves its bed and flows over the land of another the owner of the latter is to be made good out of the previous river bed (Art 563), though the state never loses its rights if the river is navigable. To be noted also is the provision for rewarding the workman for the work he does on property (Art 571) and the person who by good luck discovers treasure on the property of another (Art 716).

It is inferable from Art 543 that the only possible variants of ownership are usufruct and servitudes. As in Roman law usufruct leaves the 'substance' of the property vested in the owner (Art 578). Servitudes can be 'created by the act of man' only if they increase the utility of buildings or land. They arise from agreement, possession for 30 years (provided that their use is continuous and apparent, Art 690) or 'decision of the paterfamilias' (Art 692): to avoid disputes between neighbours rights were not to arise from 'conduct which was equivocal'. In their concern to prevent any revival of the former divisions of ownership the codifiers laid down that no other rights could exist as real rights, but they did not follow through the revolutionary logic of article 544, for they mention 'real rights' in connection with mortgage (Art 2114) and as to the 'modifications of ownership', they allude in Art 553 to the possibility of having one person owning the building on land belonging to another.

Section 2: Transferring, using and securing property

Book Three of the *Code civil* is entitled 'On the different methods of acquiring ownership', and proceeds from sections on succession and gift to the sizeable field of *obligations*, consisting of contractual obligations, the subject-matter of the lengthy general title (Arts 1101–1369), and obligations which arise without agreement, treated more cursorily in Arts 1370–1386, both of which lead to the acquisition or transfer of ownership (I). The special contracts which are covered in titles VI to XIII of Book Three are also ways of transferring or using things (II). Finally, there are those institutions (sureties, pledges, charges and hypothecs) whose natural function is to render ownership more secure (III).

I. Obligations subserving ownership

Having decided against including a 'general part' which could have dealt with acts-in-law, the draftsmen nevertheless offer in Title III of Book Three 'a body of elementary doctrine having both the precision and the authority of law' (A). Title IV on other types of obligation is also quite general, whereas the following titles deal with special types of contract and are more specific (B). In these areas the 'written reason' of Roman law and natural equity are pressed into service in order to 'maintain the order of society' (Treilhard) and 'safeguard the wealth of individuals' (Favard).

A. The binding force of contracts

'Obligation' is not defined in the *Code civil*, but 'contract', following Pothier, is described as 'an agreement whereby one or more persons bind themselves, as against one or more others, to do or not to do something' (Art 1101). We are then told that contracts may be either synallagmatic or unilateral and either gratuitous or for reward, but the general conception is broad and eschews the Roman distinction between nominate contracts and those with no name (Art 1107), while reserving some special rules for 'commercial transactions'.

'There are four essential conditions for the validity of a contract' (Art 1108). By putting consent first, the codifiers stress the importance of 'the meeting of the intentions of all the parties at interest' (Treilhard). Since consent must be free, mistake, duress and fraud give rise to rescission, though not to absolute nullity. In principle one cannot bind oneself or the other contractor to a third party (Art 1119), except in specified cases and when the promise to render a benefit to the third party has been accepted by him (Art 1121). Other conditions for the validity of a contract are the *capacity* of the parties, the *object* ('things in commerce,' identified by the kind of things they are), and a *cause*. 'Cause' is not defined in the Code, but according to Bigot de Préameneu it is constituted by 'the reciprocal interest of the parties or the intention of one of them to benefit the other'; it need not be expressed in the contract but it must exist and must not be 'contrary to good morals or the public interest' (Art 1133). Here 'public order' and 'good morals', already mentioned in Art 6, mark the limits of freedom of contract.

Consent, the primary requirement in the Code, is normally sufficient in itself: only a few contracts are subject to a particular formality (marriage, gift, mortgage) and writing is necessary only where the object of the contract exceeds 150 francs in value, a rule taken straight from pre-revolutionary law. But if many types of contract can be made orally and evidenced by witnesses or oath (Art 1333 refers to 'tallies', the notched sticks traditionally used by bakers), contractual rights are not the product of private autonomy alone. Following Domat and in the spirit of Roman law Art 1134 provides that only contracts 'formed in accordance with the law' have 'the force of law' between the parties, an article which the Tribune Favard explained as showing that a contract 'was the result of the law itself', adding that, as Art 1135 shows, customary practice no less than the law has a role in determining the content of contracts.

As to the effect of contracts, the promisor must perform his promise in good faith. In particular, where there is an 'obligation to transfer' the creditor becomes owner of the promised thing by consent alone without any need for actual delivery (Art 1142). There are many ways in which the debtor can free himself from the obligation (payment, set-off, merger of obligations, novation, waiver, composition), and the courts may offer further protection by limiting the damages payable for delay or non-performance. As against this, contracts may validly contain penalty clauses (Art 1126) and the *Code civil* even reinforced the obligations of some undeserving debtors, such as farmers and merchants and those offering security without revealing existing charges (*stellionat*) by threatening them with imprisonment (Arts 2059–2070).

B. Non-consensual obligations

After dealing with the discharge of consensual obligations (without making a clear distinction between obligation, agreement and contract) the codifiers devoted only 17 articles to obligations arising without any consent or agreement between the parties. Art 1370 distinguishes between obligations which 'arise by the sole authority of the law' (such as those of neighbours and tutors) and those which 'arise from the act of the individual who is bound' and are covered in the following articles. Despite references to natural equity these obligations, arising from quasi-contracts, delicts and quasi-delicts, obtain their force from the law, for the law 'wants us to want what we would want if we were just' (Treilhard).

Quasi-contracts result from lawful human conduct, the Code concentrating on the effects of the management of another person's affairs (*gestion d'affaires*, Arts 1372–1375). Wary of the overzealous intervener, the Code requires him to behave as a 'good family man' in looking after the property of the owner. The law is even more severe when a person receives money or property which was not due to him, especially if he was in bad faith (Art 1378): 'these obligations arise from the principle that there should be no transfer of ownership in property without some legitimate ground' (Tarrible).

The chapter on delicts and quasi-delicts starts out with the famous article: 'Every act whatever of man that cause damage to another obliges him by whose fault the damage arose to repair it' (Art 1382). 'Fault' is not defined, though Art 1383 states that a person is responsible not only for his act ('*fait*' – alluding to intentional fault as delictual?) but also for his 'negligence' or 'imprudence'. Responsibility is then extended to include not only 'those for whom one is answerable' – thus mothers and fathers are answerable for their minor children, masters and employers for servants and employees, teachers and workmen for their students and apprentices – but also 'things under one's control', owners of animals or buildings which collapse being made liable for the damage they cause.

Some explanations of these very terse articles on which the law of civil responsibility was to be based were offered by those who spoke for the government or in the Tribunate. The extremely comprehensive formula ('every act whatever of man') was designed to make individuals (including, according to the spokesmen, the spendthrift) 'warrant their conduct', fault being a 'failure of self-control' and answer for every 'unlawful act' (Tarrible) – that is, any act which 'harms the rights of others' (Bertrand de Greuille). Monetary reparation of all damage (except 'the work of fate') is called for by public order and the 'preservation of property of all kinds'. Delicts are seen 'exclusively from the viewpoint of the person whose interests are injured' (Tarrible), for 'the law cannot treat in the same way the person at fault and the person who suffers' (Bertrand de Greuille).

But Arts 1382–1386 should not lead us to suppose that they are concerned only with the rights of individuals. As well as being a 'civil guarantee' of the property of others they constitute an important incentive 'to vigilance on the part of those with the sacred office of authority' such as fathers and mothers, masters and employers, and teachers and artisans. Their liability will 'focus attention on the conduct of those in their charge' and 'prevent any relaxation of domestic discipline' (Tarrible). Logically enough, the liability of parents ceases when the children leave the family home and that of masters and employers arises only as regards the functions for which their employees and servants are engaged. But whereas parents, teachers and artisans can escape liability by proving that they could not prevent the conduct which did the damage, masters and employers are more strictly liable, seeing that they profit from the service rendered. In this way the law sees to it that 'the owner, the artist, the tradesman can devote themselves with confidence and assurance to their domestic cares, their creative work and their enterprises'.

II. Special contracts subserving ownership

Art 1107 heralds the 'detailed rules' which apply to contracts according to their type. After the contract of marriage, which we have covered in relation to matrimonial property regimes, come sale (A) and services (B) – to which the legislator paid particular attention, the relevant titles having more than 100 articles. Other less common contracts which contribute less to the acquisition of wealth receive shorter and more traditional treatment; some of them involve a counterpart (C), some are gratuitous (D).

A. Sale – *freedom and control*

The codifiers regarded sale as the most important of all contracts; indeed, according to Grenier, without it 'one could hardly imagine civilisation at all'. Said to originate in the transaction of exchange (Arts 1702–1707), it is consensual and informal, writing being required only as evidence (Art 1582). Even if 'it is consent and reliance which makes the contract' (Portalis), it must be regulated by the legislature and supervised by the administration since it can pander to 'human greed and ambition' and affects the disposition of 'family assets' and the 'wealth of the citizen'. Important points are whether a contract of sale operates as a conveyance and whether it can be rescinded for lesion (where the price is much less than the value). As to the former, once there is agreement on the thing (provided it is saleable, Art 1598) and the price (which must be fixed, Art 1591) the sale is said to be 'complete between the parties' (a formula which leaves unanswered the question whether third parties can object): unlike in Roman law, there is no need for delivery of the thing or payment of the price (Art 1583). As to lesion, if 'the will of man, supported by the full force of law, neutralises distance and overcomes all obstacles, like the law itself' it is not all-powerful, because there are 'rules of justice' which must 'control what is agreed'. Although rescission of sales for lesion was abolished by the Law of 31 August 1795 (14 *fructidor* year III) (owing to the chaos resulting from inflation) the *Code civil* reinstated it 'if the seller of land received less than seven-twelfths of its value' (Art 1674) and sues within two years. The 'just price' is to be established by experts, and rescission is limited to sales of land, for such sellers are assumed to sell at an undervalue only because of pressure of affairs. Dealings in movables were in principle free, though rules of the *Code civil* indicated a concern, actualised in 1807 in the *Code de commerce*, to 'ensure probity in commercial dealings'.

B. Hire and services

'The contract of hire and other services comes immediately after that of sale' (Galli). It is therefore subject to general rules akin to those of sale: consent on the thing to be hired and the price are sufficient, and the contract may be made in writing or orally (Art 1714). This is as in Roman law, but the Code deviates from Roman law in a certain number of respects, applicable to all contracts of hire of property, in particular as regards the period required for notice (depending, in the absence of writing, on local practice, Art 1736), the tenant's right to remain despite sale by the landlord (unless the lease provides otherwise, Art 1743) and the inability of the landlord, failing a contrary stipulation in the lease (Art 1761), to cancel the lease because he wants to use the property himself.

The rules of lease differ according to whether the object is a house, a chattel or land in the country. In addition to the lease of agricultural land in its proper sense the general term '*bail à ferme*' in the *Code civil* covers share-cropping (*métayage*) where the rent takes the form of part of the crop (a case where the Code prohibits subleasing). These contracts may be formed for several years at a time or for one year only (in the absence of writing Art 1774 lays down presumptions) and in principle they terminate on the expiry of the period agreed (Art 1775). Strict obligations are laid on the lessee of rural land: he must take care of the land like the 'good father of a family' (Art 1766) and make it easier for his successor to take over the farm (Art 1777). In the lease of cattle, covered in Arts 1800–1817, the terms also favour the owner.

Different distinctions are drawn where a person takes on a task or agrees to work for another. The employment of domestic servants and workmen must be limited either in time or in terms of the task in question (Art 1780), for if it were open-ended this would conflict with the 'principle of individual liberty' (Mouricault). Where there is a dispute over whether the right wage has been paid (Art 1781) 'the solemn word of the employer is to be believed' because he is 'more trustworthy' (Treilhard). 'Carriers by land or water' are subject to special obligations regarding the safety of their cargoes. Where a person works on material supplied by a customer, there is another deviation from Roman law: under Art 1790 the workman has no right to any payment if the thing supplied by the customer is accidentally lost, on the ground that the workman, being 'owner' of his work, must bear the risk of its loss (Mouricault). It is characteristic of this contract that the owner-customer wins out over the person doing the work: equally favourable to owners are Arts 1792 and 1793 which respectively render architects and developers liable for a period of 10 years and prohibit any unilateral increase in the price.

C. Mutually beneficial contracts

Partnership (Art 1832) is a contract of mutual advantage since it is with a view to sharing the benefits that the parties enter into an agreement to pool their property or industry (as distinct from a mere loan). Although the rules on partnership in the Code are quite general they do not apply to commercial companies, which were to be subject to special rules in future codes (Art 1873). The codifiers disregarded the *société taisible* of prior law, an informal agreement to share property, for which evidence in writing was required, and saw partnership not as a combination of capital but rather as a temporary association in view of a purchase or lease or common adventure or 'any kind of business' (Treilhard), an association of persons based on 'mutual trust'. Partnerships of all property are viewed with some suspicion: they cannot include future acquisitions lest they might be donations in disguise (Art 1836). As to the legal personality of the partnership, which terminates in principle on the death of any of the parties (absent a contrary stipulation, Art 1868) or renunciation (Art 1869), the *Code civil* is silent – though some, such as the Tribune Gillet, spoke of a 'collective being'.

The *Assemblée Constituante* had decided, as against the traditional view of canon law, that a lender might charge interest, and this was confirmed in the *Code civil*, thereby allowing speculation by capitalists. Despite the return to monetary stability (Art 1895 is based on the nominalist principle), the codifiers were conscious of the risk of 'excesses' of usury and did not break entirely with the tradition of a directed economy: Art 1907 enables the government to fix a statutory rate of interest, depending on the type of business involved, and envisages a prohibition of excessive rates of interest.

The same suspicion of 'ignoble commercialism' underlies the brief provisions on aleatory contracts: sums won under such contracts cannot be claimed in court. The *Code civil* leaves insurance to maritime law (Art 1964), life assurance being disliked by Portalis because of his view that the death of a human being should not be 'the object of commercial speculation'.

D. Gratuitous contracts

Alongside these contracts of mutual benefit there are several special contracts in the Code which are said to be gratuitous. These include *deposit* (Art 1917), divided into voluntary deposit, deposit in emergency (in cases of fire, pillage and shipwreck, or with hoteliers and innkeepers), and deposit by way of sequestration or escrow where the object is the subject of a dispute. The rules, taken from Roman law, impose on the depositee a duty to behave with extreme probity (the 'good man') but the codifiers also wanted to support public order: the rather strict liability of hoteliers and innkeepers (Art 1792) was thought to deter thefts and give business to the security industry.

Mandate is also a naturally gratuitous contract, an 'office of friendship' (Art 1986), 'admirably characterised by altruism and generosity' (Tarrible), but it is not neglectful of the needs of business. For example, a married woman is in principle incapable of contracting, but she may act as her husband's agent so as to facilitate the management of the household, at any rate when the husband is away. Furthermore, the agent may be authorised to receive payment, for which he remains accountable. Despite the observation of Bertrand de Greuille that gratitude should come from 'the heart and not the purse', a reward for services rendered is quite compatible with the institution of mandate.

Other acts 'of generosity, friendship or kindness' (Bouteville) include *commodatum*, or loan for use (Art 1876), as well as the interest-free loan for consumption. Here, too, the law reminds the borrower of his duties as 'good family man' and to look after the interests of the owner. One can thus see that all the special contracts are founded on the needs and reciprocal interests of those in society.

III. Securing property

Contracts may well depend on mutual trust, but the codifiers were clearly uneasy about relying on good faith alone, and sought to protect the property of creditors more securely. For private – as opposed to commercial – affairs they regarded ownership, especially ownership of land, as the measure of solvency. The debtor is liable to the extent of 'all his movable and immovable property, present and future' (Art 2092). According to the Tribune Gary 'there is greater security in things than in people'. That is why suretyship itself is based on real securities (A), why any type of property may serve as security (B), and why the debates on the system of mortgages were so heated (C).

A. Suretyship and the circulation of capital

The Code starts out with suretyship. It is simple, useful and flexible. It can be altruistic (the debtor need not even be aware of it, Art 2014), as when a 'kind parent' or 'friendly neighbour' uses it to help out a 'family in difficulties', or it can conduce to the 'circulation of capital' and the 'progress of industry'. Depending on its terms the liability of the surety can be more or less severe. In principle he can invoke the 'benefit of discussion' (whereby the creditor must first look to the principal debtor, Art 2021) and the 'benefit of division' (whereby the debt is divided between all the guarantors, Art 2026), but he may waive such rights and render himself fully liable.

This personal suretyship is closely linked in the Code to real security. The guarantor who invokes the benefit of discussion must tell the creditor what property of the debtor can be seized within the jurisdiction of the court of appeal and must offer an indemnity for the costs. Unless the debt is very small or commercial, the solvency of the guarantor must be backed by 'landed property free of charges' (Art 2019). In sum, personal suretyship is not very far removed from real security.

B. Pledge

The Code uses the term '*nantissement*' to cover both pledge of movables and *antichresis* as regards land. In both cases the creditor can take possession of the debtor's property. The rules on pledge do not apply to commercial matters nor to pawnbrokers (Art 2084). In the event the debt remains unpaid the creditor is not allowed to forfeit the property, but must go to court for an order that he may keep the item at a value fixed by experts or at auction (Art 2078). The pledge-creditor's claim primes those of other creditors.

Not only are the rules on pledge made applicable also to incorporeal movables, such as debts (Art 2075), but the codifiers finally accepted the institution of *antichresis*, which permits the creditor to take the income from landed property, an extension of the range of pledge interests which did not impinge on mortgages, for in a conflict the mortgagee is preferred to the antichresis creditor.

C. Mortgages/hyopthecs

Although there was hardly any discussion of *privilèges* (that is, the claims, such as those for legal costs or funeral expenses or by a vendor not paid in time, which can attach to goods and land), the debate over the system of mortgages was very lively. The government committee was minded to return to the system of *general* mortgages which existed under the *ancien régime*, when publication was required for their extinction but not their creation, but the legislative section of the *Conseil d'État*, by a slender majority, wanted to retain the provisions of the Law of 1 November 1798 (11 *brumaire* year VII) whereby the details of mortgages had to publicly recorded. After these rules had been defended by Treilhard against Bigot de Préameneu and Tronchet, who argued that family affairs should be kept secret, a compromise was reached by Cambacérès and Portalis (who himself would have liked to return to Roman law which did not require publicity), that the need for publication should be waived in the case of legal charges which the beneficiary was incapable of recording. Bonaparte's support for this compromise was decisive.

Contractual mortgages were 'special' (Art 1129). They required notarisation but were not implied in all notarial acts (Art 2127) and affected third parties only from the date of their being recorded in the mortgage register (Art 2134). This publicity was required 'lest citizens be regularly misled into accepting as security property which had been already mortgaged to the hilt' (Treilhard). *Judicial* mortgages which applied to the landed property, actual or future, of the judgment debtor 'must also be made public by recordation'.

Statutory charges were different. They applied for the benefit of married women (on the property of the husband pursuant to the marriage contract), minors and persons under interdict (on the property of their guardian as regards his management). These mortgages were general (unless rendered special by the marriage contract or a decision of the family council, Arts 2140 and 2141), and were enforceable regardless of recordation (Art 2135), so that the failure to record them did not hurt married women, minors or persons under interdict. Husbands and guardians were, however, under a duty to record these mortgages (Art 2136) and could not create a contractual mortgage without disclosing any statutory mortgages over their property.

There are differences between contractual and statutory hypothecs as regards the method of discharge (Arts 2181–2195). Although registration was not in general required for transactions in land the person who was buying land and wanted to discharge a contractual mortgage over it had to register his contract (Art 2181), so that creditors would be notified and could claim on the price or demand the plus-value. If the charge to be discharged was a statutory one, the person acquiring the property had to display his contract in the *tribunal civil* for two months so that wives, minors and persons under interdict could make their claims known (Art 2194). Since, however, the rights of the wife would not be known until the marriage was dissolved, this system may not have proved very useful.

This system may seem incoherent, but it can be justified as an attempt to harmonise the conflicting rights of guarantors, owners and the family. The fact that legal charges were not registrable by married women, minors and persons under interdict, was attributed of their incapacity and need for protection. In his speech presenting the title on forced execution the Tribune Lahary stressed the fact that these institutions were all interconnected. The constant need to protect property made it necessary to notify the debtor: 'If you want your property to be protected, you must respect the property of others, or you yourself will be hurt as you planned to hurt them, and you will rightly be dispossessed of the property you planned to take.' At the same time the forced execution on the debtor's property had to 'respect the interests of the married woman and protect her against herself'. The 'weakness' of women, inherent in their 'nature' made it necessary to protect the wife from ruin (for she was somewhat presumed to be thriftless) and this explains the provision in Art 2208 whereby she is relieved of the need to participate in the expropriation. Thus the novel system of charges and mortgages was thought to reconcile all the interests involved and to harmonise the law of property and the law of persons.

Chapter 4: Interpretation of the Code 1804–1904

The first shots in the battle over the merits of the *Code civil*, a battle which lasted throughout the nineteenth century, were fired by observers, both French and foreign, who were hostile not only to the Code itself but also to the law of the Revolution (I). To begin with it was the provisions on family law which came under particular fire (II). Later, the Code was attacked by liberals, democrats and socialists for being unduly authoritarian (III). Thus after being considered too innovative, even anarchic, the Code was reviled for being old-fashioned and unreflective of new ideas.

Section 1: The Code under attack

I. Too revolutionary?

Conservative opponents of the Revolution saw in the *Code civil* a legal amalgam of wrong-headed and dangerous ideas. Since such critics were hostile to Napoleon and could hardly express themselves freely in France or anywhere subject to French control, their spokesmen during the Consulate and the Empire were found among *émigrés* such as Montlosier (A), or in Germany, where Rehberg's book reflected the growth of nationalism (B) and Savigny published his views on codification (C).

A. Montlosier's proleptic criticism

In 1801, even before the Code was finalised and only the proposals of the governmental committee and the *Discours préliminaire* had been published, the Count of Montlosier (1755–1838), who had been a member of the *Constituante* before emigrating to London in 1794, published an article in the *Courrier de Londres*. This was in response to an invitation to the public for their views on codification, and his '*Observations sur le projet de Code civil*' is a good example of the kind of ideas entertained by *émigrés*, sometimes anticipating those of the ultraroyalists of the Restoration and Savigny's Historical School.

Montlosier was inclined to sympathise with the draftsmen of the government project and so did not dismiss the draft *Code civil in toto*, but thought that the primacy of the *family* as the fundamental institution of society must be reinstated and that the conditions for this were less than ideal until there was a Restoration. He criticised the draftsmen for undue deference to the ideas of the Revolution and to 'the philosophical bias of the final years of the monarchy' prevalent in the *salons* whose morals he detested. At the same time he sketched out a theory to the effect that law, rather like language, emerges as a result of natural progression in the way people actually behave, a theory which considerably reduces the role of legislation.

In what he saw as the confused 'amalgam' of prior law and Revolutionary law Montlosier singled several matters out for criticism: the concept of property, whose reference to the 'needs' of people he believed to be prejudicial to social order, the treatment of marriage as a mere contract, which led to consequences such as divorce, the law's interference with the power of the father, and the restrictions on the freedom of the head of the family to leave his property as he chose. Montlosier may sometimes be superficial in his criticisms of the 'mistakes' of the codifiers in subordinating the ownership of the head of the family to that of his dependants, but most of his themes were later taken up by the Code's conservative critics.

B. Rehberg incites people against the Code

The Hanoverian August Wilhelm Rehberg (1757–1836), an intellectual politician of counter-revolutionary stamp like Edmund Burke, made a name for himself from 1793 onwards as a violent opponent of the ideas of the French Revolution, objecting in particular to the Revolutionaries' obsession with treating everyone equally. In 1814 when the *Code Napoléon* had been introduced into Germany he published a book on it (*Über den Code Napoléon und dessen Einführung in Deutschland*) criticising the application on German territory of a foreign Code permeated with the rationalist principles of individuals who sought to 'reform the human race'. Contrary to the views of the natural lawyers he believed that law originated in custom and was gradually modified as it was transmitted from one generation to the next.

Rehberg accepted that Bonaparte and his lawyers had moderated the excesses of the Revolutionary lawyers, but nevertheless criticised the 'monstrous' idea of civil death (aimed at the *émigrés*), the treatment of marriage as merely a civil contract, the weakening of paternal power and the prohibition of paternity suits, as well as inconsistencies in the rules on succession and mortgages. While Rehberg's purpose was to keep the *Code Napoléon* out of Germany, his criticisms were echoed by contemporaries elsewhere, as in Austria (by Zeiller, who drafted the Austrian Civil Code, the ABGB) and Italy (by Negri, 1815).

C. Savigny against codification

Friedrich-Carl von Savigny (1779–1861), professor at the University of Berlin from 1810, was a distinguished Romanist, quite familiar with the work of Rehberg. When Thibaut, a professor at Heidelberg, wrote in favour of Germany's having a civil code, Savigny took issue with him and published a little work in 1814 entitled *Vom Beruf unsrer Zeit für Gesetzgebung und Rechtswissenschaft* (Is This a Good Time for Legislation and Legal Science?). This was both a statement of his historical theory of law and a criticism of the three codes then in force, the *Code Napoléon*, the Prussian Code of 1794 and the Austrian ABGB of 1811.

After delineating his ideas on the origin of law as arising from the common consciousness of the people and then being developed scientifically by jurists, Savigny states that conditions are very rarely favourable to the production of a good code. He took the history of Roman law to show that codification coincides with decadence, and did not see the circumstances in the Germany of his day as propitious for the creation of a civil code. Of the *Code Napoléon* Savigny is severely critical. He thought it was a hasty piece of work, produced as political support for Napoleon's despotic ambition, technically rather mediocre, admittedly drafted by true jurists (the four members of the government committee) but spoiled by the legal 'dilettantes' in the *Conseil d'État*. Savigny points out mistakes made by Portalis and Maleville on several questions of Roman Law, and while acknowledging the merits of Pothier he draws a rather gloomy picture of the state of legal science in France, though he modified his views somewhat in his second edition.

Savigny's criticisms of the technical aspects of the *Code civil* are more subtle than those of Rehberg, especially as regards its structure and lacunae, the absence of definitions and lack of clear general principles on property and obligations. In the treatment of nullity in marriage and contracts he sees an example of the intellectual confusion of the codifiers: several articles contradicted each other and too much was left to the discretion of the courts. He infers from this that the codifiers had no theory of the sources of law, because they were so persuaded of the omniscience of the legislation that they failed to say which subsidiary sources could be resorted to where there was a gap in it. He noted that natural law had never played much of a role in France and predicted that, contrary to the aims of the Code itself, there would be confusion if different courts of appeal felt free to revert to prior law under the guise of invoking equity or natural law.

Savigny's criticisms of the *Code civil* had less effect in France than his historical view of the way law develops. His views were made available after the Restoration, mainly through the periodical *La Thémis*, founded by Jourdan, who himself thought that the *Code Napoléon* should not have been produced until politics had stabilised but never suggested that there was anything wrong with the idea of codification as such.

II. Destructive of the family?

In France, to begin with, the principal critics of the *Code civil* were conservatives convinced that the family was the essential foundation of society. These thinkers of the counter-revolutionary and liberal right saw the *Code Napoléon* as endorsing the individualist ideas of the Revolution and the Enlightenment and endangering the stability and integrity of the family by introducing divorce, restricting paternal power and enforcing the principle of equality in intestate succession. These views of the ultraroyalists and legitimists of the first half of the nineteenth century (A) were taken up and developed by the proponents of 'reform' – 'moral' or 'social' (B).

A. The view of ultraroyalists and legitimists

The counter-revolutionary and conservative ideology of the family was a reaction to Revolutionary legislation, especially to the introduction of divorce by the law of 20 September 1792. In the early decades of the nineteenth century royalists focussed on family law without really taking a view of the *Code civil* as a whole. Thus in *Du divorce*, published in 1801 after his return to France incognito under the Directorate, the Viscount de Bonald (1754–1840) vigorously opposed the institution of divorce, and credited Portalis and Maleville with views broadly similar to his own. He conceded that the draft then under discussion did something towards re-establishing the power of the husband and father, but found the provisions on divorce unacceptable and inconsistent with the intentions of the draftsmen. Once the Restoration had taken place all the efforts of Bonald and the ultraroyalists were directed towards procuring the abolition of divorce, and this was soon achieved by the Law of 8 May 1816. By contrast there was little support, even among the ultraroyalist majorities in the assemblies, for the proposals made by certain churchmen, deputies and judges (including Chrestien de Poly) that the register of births, marriages and deaths be returned to the church and that disinhersion be reintroduced.

If the jurists of the legitimist right refrained from mounting a sustained attack on the *Code civil* as a whole, there was one author who never stopped censuring it: Honoré de Balzac. In *Le Curé du village* (1841) he criticised the individualism of the Code ('discretion and equality') as destructive of 'the family of yore', and he was particularly severe on the law of succession, 'the great scourge of France', 'the pestle breaking up the countryside'. In *Le Contrat de marriage* (1835) he had deplored the way the Code 'put the wife under guardianship' and 'treated her as a minor'. These examples confirm that the family, and particularly the law of succession, was in the forefront of the legitimists' complaints.

B. Conservative criticism continued

The theme of 'defence of the family', so dear to the legitimist, was picked up again in the second half of the nineteenth century by an engineer and sociologist called Frédéric Le Play (1806–82). In *La Réforme sociale en France*, which appeared in 1864 at the beginning of the Second Empire, he criticised the 'forcible' division of estates on death, which he attributed to the 'Laws of the Terror'. While conceding that the *Code civil* had to some extent 'softened' it, the system nevertheless 'remained in thrall to the sad theory that the State was entitled to destroy the family'. He therefore complained not only of the beggarly amount of which the testator was free to dispose and the rules which prevented the formation of landholdings of sensible size, but also of the weakening of the marriage bond (transformed into a race for the dowry) and the failure to sanction seducers, resulting from the prohibition on paternity suits (Art 340). In *L'Organisation du travail* (1870) he amplified these criticisms of the 'work of destruction' which revolutionary law had wrought on the sound tradition of customary law, especially the 'disorder' resulting from seduction, and in *L'Organisation de la famille* (1871) he narrated the history of a stock family, the Mélougas, in an attempt to show by way of factual example how the *Code civil* can ruin modest properties and reduce the birthrate.

At the turn of the century Le Play's opinions were taken up and vigorously defended. Some of his arguments were used by right-wing groups to show that the Revolution and the *Code civil* were responsible for the decadence of France, made manifest in the defeat by Prussia in 1870–71. The conservative view that the *Code civil* was one of the 'roots of the evil' was reinforced by Renan (1823–92) whose attacks on the unduly materialist and individualist tendencies of the 'Code of the Revolution' are contained in his *Essais de morale et de critique*, first published in 1868. The topics principally targeted by the critics were the rules on succession and paternal power and the prohibition on paternity suits, which Charles Jacquier, a catholic advocate, attacked as 'cruel' in 1874. The criticisms were summarised in *La France et le Code Napoléon* (1894) by J.-B.-V. Coquille, a journalist who accused the *Code civil* of conducing to poverty, turning citizens into 'slaves of the state', facilitating immigration, enriching the Jews by permitting usury, and eviscerating the ownership of the father of the family. Of course this antirepublican, xenophobic and anti-Semitic diatribe went overboard, but it does show the effect, even on the liberal right, of some of the arguments of Le Play and his school.

III. Authoritarian?

Later in the nineteenth century a broad range of thinkers claiming to be liberal and egalitarian criticised the Code as being unduly authoritarian. The liberals in particular suspected that it hindered economic development (A), and although not many republicans attacked the Code (B), the socialists regarded it as 'bourgeois' (C) and the feminists saw it as oppressing women (D).

A. Concerns of the liberals

Liberal thinkers in France were not very interested in the Code as such. Many of them, like Benjamin Constant, were reassured by its apparent respect for private life and the way it allowed the father of the family to supervise his children, while Tocqueville, in his *De la démocratie en Amérique* (2nd edn., 1840) seemed more disturbed by the 'populist' and 'democratic' principles in the Code's treatment of property and the family. Like many of his contemporaries Tocqueville disapproved of the limitations on the father's power to dispose of his property and contrasted it with the total freedom of testation in the United States. In 1865 a liberal economist called Courcelle-Seneuil also criticised the Code's rules on the disposable part, and described the Code as an 'ad hoc compromise between parties exhausted by faction and incapable of understanding each other'.

Some less well-known liberal writers were more severely critical of the Code and favoured its revision. In 1836–1837 Pellegrino Rossi (1787–1848) stated that the *Code civil* caused 'some difficulties' in the 'body social', and was more unhappy about its gaps than its method and draftsmanship: in his view it ignored the income from capital and enterprise, underestimated the importance of movable property and hampered the growth of credit by its provisions on legal charges and imprisonment for debt. In addition to opposing the dowry system, a memorandum by Batbie (1865) focussed on the provisions of the Code which he alleged to be inconsistent with the principles of ownership and freedom of contract: 'political economy has shown that the Code was unduly regulatory'. Joubaire's *Essai sur la révision du Code civil* (1873) also took against rules such as those on loans at interest which were thought to limit the rights of individuals. In sum the liberals tended to mute their criticisms on the law of persons in order to concentrate their fire on economic matters, the law of property and obligations, on the view that they gave too much power to the state.

B. A militant republican voice

Most republican jurists refrained from denigrating the *Code Napoléon*, but Émile Acollas (1826–91) is an exception. He attacked it relentlessly, and kept on denouncing it as 'a piece of work bearing the stamp from the outset of a new onslaught by the state on freedom of discussion' (*Nécessité de refondre l'ensemble de nos codes*, 1866). He held that the codal provisions on marriage, paternal power, ownership and succession were all in conflict with democratic principles and the autonomy of the individual. The Code was 'formally unjust' to married women, reduced the illegitimate child to the status of a pariah, and treated the ill-mannered child as a 'criminal'; it had limited the rights of the owner in favour of the administration or his descendants and made many mistakes regarding obligations. Its mode of government was no better than that of a 'common sergeant-major', and it had 'entrenched the counter-revolution in the very core of civil society' (*Manuel de droit civil*, 1869).

The violence of Acollas's arguments may have found favour with a few republican opponents of the Second Empire but it had no followers under the Third Republic, and although his very personal views were not too far away from certain liberal ideas concerning property and successions, they had little influence on those of a socialist or feminist persuasion.

C. A 'bourgeois code'?

Karl Marx believed that the French Revolution constituted a victory 'of private law over medieval privileges', but that private property had subsequently become 'the right of the egoist'. In 1849 he wrote that the *Code Napoléon* was the 'expression in law of the bourgeois society', a society doomed soon to disappear. Socialist thinkers in France, both forerunners such as Saint-Simon and Fourier, and supporters of labour, such as Louis Blanc and the Marxists, tended to take against the entire legal system, which was supposed to have destroyed the families of workmen by binding them to an unfairly prejudicial contract. The phrase 'bourgeois code' does not appear until surprisingly late – in the work of a liberal conservative, Ernest Glasson (1839–1907), Dean of the Paris Faculty of Law and author of several works from 1886 to 1900 on the *Code civil* and on labour matters. He was echoed in 1898 when the Belgian advocate Edmond Picard characterised the *Code Napoléon* as 'the Code of bourgeois and capitalist individualism' (*L'Évolution historique du droit civil français*).

But socialist criticism of the *Code civil* did not really find a spokesman until Maxime Leroy, whose thesis, *L'Esprit de la législation napoléonienne* (1898) maintains that the Code, inspired by authoritarian ideas, was a 'capitalist and bourgeois organ whose illiberal provisions were in conflict with the individualism of the 18th century'. The fact that the Code is silent on labour contracts he attributes not to ignorance of industry and its workforce but to a deliberately inegalitarian policy of separating men from their fellow-men. In sum he regarded the *Code civil* as 'transitional', and maintained that it had failed to promote social peace. Leroy developed his views in 1904 in *Le Code civil et le droit nouveau*, seeking to undermine the 'legend' of the Code by saying that the draftsmen 'used their work for self-glorification'. In addition to his criticism of the way the Code regulated property Leroy held that it was 'law for the father and the husband', but like many other socialists he did not separate out the problem of women from the general problem of industrial relations.

D. Targeted by feminists

As the numbers in the feminist movement grew and its organisation improved during the nineteenth century it came to oppose the provisions in the *Code civil* on the family and on women in particular. From 1836 to 1838 the *Gazette des femmes*, one of the first feminist journals, accused the Code of having taken away some of the rights which women had enjoyed under the *Ancien régime* and demanded the revision of certain articles, in particular those on the dowry regime and the wife's obligation to obey her husband. By 1878 militant reformers had begun to organise conferences and issue manifestoes, in one of which Maria Desraismes stated 'So far as women are concerned the Code is nothing but a long list of the humiliations and servitudes they are made to suffer throughout their life.' The brothers Margueritte saw it as 'a man's Code, made by men for men', and Hubertine Auclert, who habitually interrupted the reading of the *Code civil* at weddings in Paris town halls, marked the centenary of the Code in 1904 by burning a copy of it at the foot of the column in the Place Vendôme, an act which symbolises the passions which the Code was still able to inflame 90 years after Rehberg and Savigny. It must, however, be remembered that the Code had had its devoted supporters and been treated as sacred for several generations.

Section 2: The Code defended and interpreted

According to Bigot de Préameneu the *Code civil* of 1804, glorified by Napoleon's propaganda and renamed the *Code Napoléon* in 1807, came to be regarded with 'religious awe' as a kind of 'ark of the covenant'.

Even when the Empire came to an end with the Restoration there developed a veritable cult which treated the Code as a 'masterpiece' (I). Most lawyers in France not only defended their 'juristic Bible' against its assailants but continually revitalised it by their interpretative exposition (II).

I. Apologia for a masterpiece

Depending on their aims and preferences, some of the Code's defenders praised its form, others its content: it was lauded for its style and clarity (A), for its political and social value (B), and often for its consonance with morality and religion as they were understood in the nineteenth century (C).

A. Formal and technical quality

The draftsmanship of the Code was praised at an early stage, and one of the first to speak of it with fervour was the German Zachariae von Lingenthal, professor at Heidelberg (*Handbuch des französischen Civilrechts*, 1808). He called it a model of draftsmanship, 'on the whole remarkable', notwithstanding some reservations, mainly on the borrowings from Revolutionary law. Zachariae must have approved of the French codifiers for not trying to produce a work of legal science such as the authors of the Prussian Code strove for. Another professor at Heidelberg, Thibaut, likewise regarded the *Code civil* as a model of clarity and precision, full of good ideas, and made it clear in a manual published posthumously in 1841 that he was not one of his fellow-countrymen who praised the Code only in order to flatter Napoleon after his victory at Jena. In England, too, in the 1820s Jeremy Bentham, a devotee of codification, praised the *Code Napoléon* above all for trying to be as complete as possible.

In France the style of the *Code civil* met with approval from Stendhal who wrote in a letter to Balzac in 1840 '[W]hile writing *La Chartreuse* I used to read two or three pages of the *Code civil* every morning in order to perfect my own style'. Lawyers were also prompt to praise the technical merits of the 'immortal creation' (Proudhon), citing its 'luminous simplicity' (Troplong, *De la vente*, 1834), and its qualities of unity, method, precision and clarity (Planiol). Even those who found fault with the structure of the *Code civil* – such as Marcadé on the law of obligations in the 1840s – spoke of 'a great and beautiful piece of work' or 'system' (Lerminier).

B. Political and social quality

As the Napoleonic legend bloomed during the nineteenth century the view of the *Code civil* as sacred was much enhanced by the historians of

Revolution and Empire. Thus Mignet in 1841 regarded the Code as 'the most reasonable, clearest and most just law of any country yet', and especially praised the way the codifiers clung to 'the spirit of the Revolution'. In his view the *Code Napoléon* liberated workmen, established that children must be treated equally, and contributed to the extension and propagation of property. In 1844 he repeated his admiration for a Code 'so solidly conceived, so simply constructed, so clearly written and so wisely and generously regulating the status of the citizen'. He saw in it the 'imprescriptible charter of civil rights'.

Similar ideas were developed by Adolphe Thiers in his *Histoire du Consulat et de l'Empire* (1849) where he too speaks of the Code as an 'imperishable work', a 'masterpiece of legislation', a code fit for 'the modern civilised world'. For Thiers the *Code Napoléon* was an 'admirable summary of French law purged of all feudalism', which could not have been better done. It could be called the 'social code', for it conduced to the 'best form of society'. The objections raised in the Tribunate he held 'vacuous and silly', and praised the 'strong will' and 'universal spirit' of Bonaparte. Finally he thought that in attaching itself to 'principles of true equality', that is, equality before the law, the *Code civil* had reached solid ground between 'reactionary tendencies and revolutionary follies'. In 1865 the republican Edgar Quinet wrote in his history that though the Code came after the coup d'état of 18 brumaire (9 November 1799) it was a 'monument which raised law above force', similar in substance and spirit to the project put to the *Convention* in 1793. The *Code civil* would be Napoleon's 'true glory': as Napoleon himself predicted on Saint Helena, he would go down to history as the great legislator. Even the conservative historian Hippolyte Taine (1823–93) was full of admiration for the statesmanlike way each citizen was granted a 'private space', a 'zone reserved for himself' (*Les Origines de la France contemporaine*, completed in 1892).

C. Moral quality

Commentators frequently observed with particular reference to the provisions relating to the family, once divorce had been abolished in 1816, that the *Code civil* was not merely consonant with good conduct in society but also informed by the highest morality. This was an argument designed to defuse criticism. Thus in their *Cours de droit civil français*, based on the manual of Zachariae, Aubry and Rau were guilty of misrepresentation when they translated him as saying (vol. 6, §566) that the prohibition on paternity suits had no adverse effect on public morals. Demolombe was likewise ready to justify article 340 as one which is perhaps more than ever called for, given the actual state of morality in our society', and stated that the rules on paternal power were 'the constitution of civil society in France', quite in line with 'the habits of our society'. Toullier and Duranton expressed similar views on this rather contentious part of the *Code civil*.

In 1835 Lerminier, an admirer of Savigny, held that the Code was 'idealistic', free from any taint of utilitarianism and materialism (*Introduction générale à l'histoire du droit*), and Troplong went further than anyone else, in stating first that it was 'intimately linked with rational Christianity' (*De la vente*, 1834), and later describing it as 'idealistic' and 'Christian' (*Du prêt*, 1845). Here, too, the Code's supporters were responding to attacks on it as 'atheistic' and 'materialistic'. Those who praised the Code proceeded to interpret it.

II. The Lawyers' Bible interpreted

The series of analyses and commentaries on the Code stretches from Maleville and Locré (1805) through Proudhon, Toullier and Duranton in the first three decades of the century to Troplong, Demolombe, Aubry and Rau between 1830 and the start of the Third Republic. In works designed for students and practitioners these authors sought to explicate the law exegetically, usually subjecting the articles to textual analysis in the order in which they appeared, but despite their efforts to stick to the text they could not conceal their personal opinion or ignore the way ideas were developing. One can therefore identify different stages of interpretation as currents of thought changed: liberal interpretation (A), a democratic reading (B) and, at the time of the centenary of the Code in 1904, a 'national' view (C).

A. Gradually progressive interpretation

The codifiers did not use the word 'liberal' and the earliest commentators did not use it very much either. A simple passage from Locré to the effect that the *Code Napoléon* occurred at the moment 'when there was a return to good order, sound ideas, ideas that were truly grand, really liberal', shows that in 1805 'liberal ideas' were seen as guaranteeing the liberty of the citizen and were not yet thought of as a ground for countering determined political and social authoritarianism. Nor does Toullier in his *Droit civil* (2nd edn., 1819) think to explain how one could reconcile the rules of the *Code civil* with the liberty of the individual, proclaimed by the Revolution and entrenched in the Charter of 1814. His citation of ownership as one of the 'absolute rights of man' does however suggest liberalism might find its way into the interpretation of the *Code civil*.

Though Toullier considered 'imprescriptible ownership' as 'the product of private law' the writers of the 1830s and 1840s treated it more as a natural right and saw Art 544 as according the owner a sovereign liberty. This is supported after 1839 by the idea of the 'patrimony' which Aubry and Rau took from Zachariae. The Lockean origin of ownership in the Code was emphasised by Thiers and Troplong, who were afraid that the revolutionary spirit of 1848 might prove contagious. They noted the connection between ownership, liberty and work, and Demolombe, who was opposed to any restriction on the right of the owner, even that of abuse of rights, also wrote that in the Code individual property was 'work, liberty itself'.

Although private lawyers in France accepted that the *Code Napoléon* was based on the will of the individual, taking as examples the formation of contracts, the transfer of title by mere consent and liability based on fault, they did not speak of the 'autonomy of the individual will' until the end of the nineteenth century. Demolombe used the *Code civil* to show that there could be no lesion in contracts of employment and that in deciding the terms of their contracts 'the free will of the parties is sovereign'. Troplong's treatise *Des donations entre vifs et des testaments* (1855) informs the reader that the *Code civil* is the 'foundation-stone of our civil liberties' and that it 'guards all liberal combinations against intervention by a usurping state'. We can thus see liberalism creeping almost unobserved into the interpretation of the provisions of the *Code civil* on property and obligations.

B. The Code as 'democratic'

Those who first described the Code as 'democratic' did so as a criticism, because of their dislike of the way property was divided equally among descendants; this, for example, was the view of Tocqueville in 1840. Then came the revolution of February 1848, and Troplong, a distinguished judge and jurist, wrote favourably of 'the democratic spirit of the *Code civil*', and in a paper delivered at the *Institut* he associated democracy with natural law founded on ethics and equity. For him, the *Code civil*, albeit conceived at a time of 'return to good order', was 'the work of the men of the revolution', bearing 'the stamp of its democratic origins', on every page of which, according to him, equality was writ large. The provisions on the powers of the husband and father, on guardianship and interdiction were included merely to manage 'natural and inevitable inequalities' by protecting the weak (such as women) from despotism by 'humanitarian ideas'. On the rule permitting the imprisonment of an unruly child on the demand of the father Troplong did not hesitate to say '(I)t is all done without anger, without formalities, without scandal. Liberty is safeguarded, for the sanctions available to the father are limited'. He also held that the views of the codifiers on marriage were informed by pure democratic ideas, divorce being a 'concession to the perverted upper classes'. Although this exalted praise of the Code owed much to the circumstances and personal views of its author, who was to become one of Napoleon III's strongest supporters, the same concern to emphasise the egalitarianism of the *Code civil* can be found in other commentators, in part reacting to the attacks of the conservatives: in 1852, for example, 'democratic' was a word used by Demolombe to describe the Code's division of landed properties.

C. The Code as a national institution

The French as a nation have been proud of their *Code civil* ever since the first Empire, when they provided it as a model for other countries. This national pride figures both in the dithyrambs of Troplong and Thiers and in the historical works of Lerminier. As the nineteenth century turned into the twentieth, a time when there was a risk that the recent German Civil Code (BGB) might put the code of Napoleon in the shade, the 'profoundly national' character of the Code was particularly hymned. The handbooks of private law then produced (Planiol in 1899; Colin and Capitant in 1914) start out, unlike their predecessors, with a general appraisal of the Code, commending its 'wise spirit of moderation'. Planiol saw it as above all a 'law of give-and-take', while Colin and Capitant found it perhaps 'the most astonishing product of the fertile creativity of the generation of the Revolution'.

The centenary of the *Code civil* in 1904, at a time when relations between France and Germany were becoming tense, was the occasion for jurists and many other intellectuals to show their attachment to this national treasure, 'the glory of the legal mind' (Lévy-Ullmann). In his introduction to the *Livre du Centenaire* Albert Sorel held that this 'patriotic' celebration of the 'book of reason' of the French people was perfectly justified, for it had ensured the peace of society: it was a 'product of the soil', 'drawing its sap from the land of France', destined to be 'the common property of the French people'. Esmein, Vigié and Saleilles likewise emphasised the continuity between *Code civil* and the 'law of the past', and while Saleilles could talk of the 'code of the bourgeois' he also praised the 'flexibility' of the Code as a text with 'loose links and supple formulae'. The way was open to those in the twentieth century who wanted the law to evolve from and beyond the *Code civil* while preserving its symbolic value against a general redrafting.

Chapter 5: The View of Historians

Much research into the history of the Code has been done since the 1960s, doubtless prompted in part by the great reforms of family law which then took place. This research has produced a new way of looking at the *Code civil*: after all, the *Code civil* of today is very different from the *Code Napoléon* of 1804, and many of its rules are now of historical interest only. Whereas the task of practitioners was to interpret and apply the Code, historians have now sought to analyse the sources which inspired it, its theoretical underpinnings and its effect on society. They have accordingly looked to its genealogy (I), its ideology (II) and its sociology (III).

Section 1: The genealogy of the Code

The draftsmen of the *Code Napoléon* never tried to conceal their sources; indeed they often mentioned the borrowings they made from old or more recent law. As Portalis maintained, the Code could not be 'absolutely new', but had to draw on the 'rich heritage' of prior law and take account of the 'experience of the past'. Such a work of consolidation was bound to be affected by the spirit of the Enlightenment and the changes wrought during the Revolution, but one must not blindly take at face value the draftsmen's statements that they were trying to effect a compromise between the *droit coutumier* and the *droit écrit*, or between the law before the Revolution and the law after it. Their claims of parentage are sometimes dubious, so one must patiently trace the Code back to its roots in order to find out how much weight to attribute to traditional law (I) and modern law (II) respectively.

I. The weight of tradition

When critics attacked the Code as a mere 'reformulation of Roman law, ancient customs and traditional maxims' Portalis was unmoved. As one who was opposed to 'novelties in legislation', he defended both Roman law and customary law, primarily in order to reassure those who had lived under those systems and who might be dismayed by too brutal a breach with their habitual practices. In fact the draftsmen were not really trying to reconcile the differing and often quite divergent traditions of Roman and customary law; they looked to the 'French law' created from those divergent rules by the authors of the seventeenth and eighteenth centuries (A) or to the Roman law as mediated by centuries of scholarship (B).

A. French law wins through

While referring occasionally to the accusations of 'barbarism' which were levelled in the eighteenth century against many of the customs of pre-Revolutionary France, the draftsmen of the *Code civil* readily praised customary law for its 'wisdom' (Portalis) and its adaptation to 'the genius of France' (Treilhard). Of the many rules which had figured in the customs as officially written down from the sixteenth century onwards they incorporated those on paternal power, the marital community, the divisions of the kinds of property, servitudes and succession. Most of the borrowings came from the Custom of Paris (the 'new' version of 1580), but here and there one finds rules taken from other customs. Thus the institution of the *fente* in the law of succession was taken from customs in the West of France as mediated by the Law of 6 January 1794 (17 *nivôse* II), and in the principle of the equality of children which dominates the rules on legitimate succession in the *Code civil* there still breathes the 'spirit' of customary law, as applied to the property of commoners (as opposed to the nobles).

Quite apart from its borrowings from the text or spirit of the individual customs, the *Code civil* drew on the 'common customary law' which lawyers from the sixteenth century onwards had been trying to tease out as well as the 'French law' taught in universities after 1679. In the wake of Dumoulin's publications between 1530 and 1560 many jurists tried to find the points on which the different customs were in agreement and to fill in the gaps with rules taken from the Custom of Paris, case-law and Roman law. Some of these rules are presented as maxims by Loysel in his *Institutions coutumières* (1607), and can be found verbatim in the *Code civil*. The draftsmen also took material from the *Droit commun de la France* (1747) by the Parisian jurist Bourjon, including the famous words of Art 2279: 'En fait de meubles, la possession vaut titre' [As to movables, possession is as good as title]. Even more striking is the influence of the professors whose lectures on French law tried to effect a synthesis of customary law, the canon law received in France (on marriage, for example) and the royal ordinances on private law, such as those of the Chancellor Daguesseau. From Pothier, indeed, who taught at Orléans from 1749 to 1772, the draftsmen copied out whole paragraphs.

B. Roman law

Pothier included some Roman law in his writings, but it was often criticised under the Revolution, especially by Mirabeau. Was it somehow reinstated in the *Code civil*? Certainly Portalis was severe on 'authors who make bitter and trivial criticisms of Roman law' and 'comminate what they do not understand', though (like many of his contemporaries) he disapproved of certain aspects of the imperial legislation and the 'disorder' of Justinian's compilations. Furthermore the draftsmen kept saying that Roman law, despite being the 'law of alien conquerors' (Treilhard), was nevertheless valuable as 'written reason' and 'common law' (Galli), and expressed 'natural equity' when dealing with obligations and contracts. They also said that Roman law inspired some of the rules on successions and property which they put into the *Code civil*: Maleville even attributed Art 544 to Roman sources.

Today, however, we no longer accept the place of honour this accords to Roman law. First, there are many topics on which the Code deviates from Roman law, not only on issues such as paternal power and mortgages but also as regards contracts such as partnership and services. Second, the codifiers got their Roman law via Domat and Pothier, who were given to creative interpretation like all the generations of Romanists from the medieval glossators onwards. This explains why some of the codifiers' statements on Roman law are historically inaccurate, as Savigny pointed out. In fact relatively few concessions were made to the law of the former *pays du droit écrit*, and the ideas which the codifiers defended as being Roman law were almost always 'modern ideas' developed in the seventeenth and eighteenth centuries, dressed up in a toga. In any case, as elsewhere in Europe, codification marked a formal rupture with the Romanesque tradition.

II. Modern contributions

The *Code civil* is so much influenced by the law which had gone before it that it is far from easy to discern in it any really innovative technical element. It would nevertheless be an error to suppose that it is merely prior law in a different order. There is a lot in the *Code civil* which is not in Pothier. Notwithstanding the coyness or denials of the codifiers, the *Code Napoléon* can only be understood if one recognises the contribution made by the theorists of natural law (A) and takes account of its uneasy relationship with revolutionary law (B).

A. Modern natural law

It is quite tricky to evaluate the effect on the *Code civil* of thinkers on natural law such as Grotius (1589–1645) through Pufendorf, Locke and

Leibniz to Burlamaqui (1694–1748) and Christian Wolff (1670–1754). Apart from Portalis (and to a lesser extent Tronchet and Berlier) the codifiers hardly referred at all to these authors, none of whom was French, but their novel conceptions of law certainly had an influence, as research by André-Jean Arnaud has shown. The very plan of the *Code civil* reflects the reinterpretation by natural lawyers in the light of their rational individualism of the tripartite division of the *Institutes* of Justinian (persons, property, actions): persons are seen as the subjects of law, property is the right *par excellence*, and obligations are the means whereby individuals can acquire it. In addition, the codifiers borrowed from the natural lawyers such fundamental ideas as the passing of property by the mere force of contract and the obligation to pay for damage due to one's fault. Some of these ideas passed through Domat and Pothier but others were taken more directly from the writings of Grotius and Pufendorf.

Yet the *Code Napoléon* is far from being a pure product of the modern school of natural law. The very idea of 'natural law', used during the Revolution in different and sometimes contradictory senses, ran into difficulties under the Consulate, as is shown by the rejection of the preliminary book proposed by Portalis. Many of those involved in the preparation of the *Code civil* seem to have been more at home with the more practical solutions of French writers than with natural law theories. There is a marked contrast here with the Code Frédéric and the Prussian Code of 1794 which were strongly influenced by Pufendorf and Wolff. Thus the Prussian Code was following natural law thinking in Germany when it distinguished between the different classes and corporations, whereas the *Code Napoléon* reflects the revolutionaries' view of equality before the law.

B. Revolutionary law, positive or negative?

If one credits the repeated assertions of Portalis, the *Code civil* was drafted as a deliberate reaction, in the literal sense of the word, to the Revolutionary legislation on private law, which was allegedly inspired by a 'hatred of the past' and effected a 'dissolution' of society by 'extreme methods of great violence'. In order to counteract these 'dangerous innovations' and 'false systems' the *Code civil* was to effect a return to sound ideas, good order and moral conduct. Thus whereas under the Revolution divorce had become easy, the *Code Napoléon* made it difficult and troublesome; whereas the law of 2 November 1793 (12 *brumaire* year II) had equated bastards, if recognised, with legitimate children, the *Code civil* put a virtually insurmountable barrier between them; whereas the law of 6 January 1794 (17 *nivôse* year II) forbade the father to prefer any child over the others and severely restricted the amount of property of which the testator could freely dispose, this rule was reversed by the Code of 1804. Several other examples, such as mortgages and avoidance of sales for lesion, show the men of the Consulate rejecting rules of revolutionary law.

But every reaction involves a connection, and the relationship of the *Code civil* with the 'model' of revolutionary law is complex. To begin with, it is not easy even to define what is meant by revolutionary law in the private sphere: between 1789 and 1799 actual texts were rather few (mainly on family law), most proposals did not get beyond statements of principle or draft (as on adoption), and much prior law was maintained (the incapacity of married women was never abolished). When Portalis drew a distinction between the 'revolutionary laws' which he characterised as 'hostile, discriminatory and destructive' and other laws passed after 1789 it was not mere rhetoric. The codifiers certainly reacted strongly against the laws of 1792–94 but they often took up ideas presented to the Constituent Assembly of 1789–91. Then again, there are elements of continuity between the *Code civil* and the texts of the revolutionary period, for some of the revolutionary institutions were retained in 1804, however modified or gutted. The succession rights of recognised bastards were reduced but they were not denied, as they were under prior law. As to property, one can even talk of fidelity to the revolutionary model (Mirabeau spoke of the owner as 'absolute master'), and the same is true with regards to obligations, for it was the Constituent Assembly that introduced freedom of commerce and allowed lenders to charge interest. When one considers the three drafts offered by Cambacérès between 1793 and 1796, bearing in mind the about-turn after the fall of Robespierre, the revolutionary antecedents of the *Code civil* are even clearer. Some of the codifiers had themselves collaborated on these drafts, which had a considerable effect, the third especially: they structured private law in much the same way as the Code (though in the revolutionary drafts succession was always linked to property), made comparable borrowings from Pothier, defined property, and contained provisions on contracts and liability in delict which prefigure Arts 544, 1134 and 1382 of the *Code Napoléon*.

Finally, the *Code civil* effectively adopted the revolutionaries' view of the function of law. Portalis called the law 'the mother of all the citizens' to whom it owed 'equal protection'. Despite its unequal treatment of husband and wife and parent and child and, to a lesser extent, master and servant, the *Code civil*, unlike much of the Prussian Code, envisages the citizen in an abstract manner, not as belonging to an order or social group. But juridical technique cannot be separated from ideological basis, and this causes further problems of affiliation.

Section 2: The ideology of the Code

For many years the *Code civil* was considered individualist and voluntarist, even as liberal and idealist, but historians now see it rather differently. There is an authoritarian flavour in the *travaux préparatoires*, a concern to incorporate the individual into society (I). After their criticism of the Revolution Portalis and the main draftsmen of the Code turned to the question of what holds society together (II). Then one must consider the part played by ideology in a work which was to contribute to the ambitions of Napoléon (III).

I. The tone of the travaux préparatoires

Xavier Martin's work on the ideology behind the opinions ventilated by the draftsmen as they worked has shown that it was views about the nature of man (A) which led to the adoption of legal solutions restrictive of individual liberty (B).

A. Pessimism about human nature

In the view of the codifiers the individual was not naturally good and reasonable, but rather 'naturally egotistical' (Abrial), driven by appetite and passion and guided by self-interest or fear (called 'the beginning of wisdom' by Portalis). This pessimistic view of man comes largely from Condillac, who regarded man as a machine responding only to external stimuli: human will and reason being so weak, individual autonomy and responsibility could be no basis for a system of ethics or law.

The codifiers recognised that this congenital weakness was more marked in some human beings than in others: men were not naturally equal 'neither in height nor in strength, neither in energy nor in ability' (Portalis). Minors, indeed all young people, were immature, and women suffered from the qualities and defects attributable to their sex – more sensitive, no doubt, but also more inclined to fecklessness when their 'penchants' or 'fancies' (Lahary) are involved.

This view of the nature of man, widespread at the time of the Consulate, derives from a philosophical tradition reaching from Hobbes to the *idéologues* (such as Cabanis) through the eighteenth-century exponents of materialism and sensationism (such as Helvétius). It may well have been confirmed by the shock of the Revolution, especially the trauma of the Terror, for the state of nature came to be described as 'a state of barbarism and mindless violence' (Saint-Aubin). This may help to explain why people were so sceptical and dismissive of the theories of the natural lawyers who regarded men as congenitally sociable.

B. *Reconstruction of society by force of law*

Given these views of the nature of man the draftsmen of the *Code civil* wanted the law to impose constraints on the individual in the interests of society, a society which it was necessary to reconstruct and put back into order after 'the troubles which drove men out of their minds' (Albisson). In line with the view of Portalis that '[I]n law the individual is nothing, society is everything', they did not try to regenerate man but sought to utilise his defects and trade on his self-interest by occasionally giving him the illusion of liberty.

The family presented the best method of procuring this forced socialisation, but it could not be based solely or mainly on love, altruism or gratitude. No, it is out of interest that children respect their parents (Favard), and it is interest which explains adoption, so that the adoptive parent may have 'support' and 'consolation' in his old age. Since the threat of disinherison is the strongest weapon in the father's armoury, he must be able to 'reward and punish'. We need the rule that gifts between spouses can be revoked and that the division of the legal community be equal so that spouses will be more affectionate to each other and more concerned for the prosperity of the husband. The illegitimate child is to be treated as a pariah because he is not a member of the family at all.

Property is another device for attaching the individual to the order of society. This is why the draftsmen of the *Code civil* saw property not as a natural right but rather as a creation of civil society. The individual's freedom of disposition was not to be absolute, as the rules on spendthrifts show, and freedom of contract was itself limited: in place of the idea of the autonomy of the will the law introduced a system which required people with volatile minds to respect their engagements. The freedom thus conceded may lead the owner and father to 'believe that they are following their own will', but they are really in thrall to the common interest and in service to the state.

II. *The interaction of ideologies*

In discussing the ideology underlying the *travaux préparatoires* one must give pride of place to those draftsmen who were obviously concerned to give the legislative enterprise a theoretical foundation. Here Portalis stands out, by virtue of his wide culture and his contacts with the intellectual movements of his time (A). The other draftsmen rarely cite their sources, but their occasional opinions support the view that at the time the *Code civil* was being produced the great ideologies of the nineteenth century were beginning to emerge and interact (B).

A. Portalis the eclectic

Although one should not overestimate the influence of Portalis on the *Code civil*, since he was quite often in a minority, nor exaggerate the coherence of his thinking, since it varied according to the circumstances, as a theorist he was nevertheless clearly superior to his collaborators. One of his numerous addresses, the *Discours préliminaire*, is justly famous, but while he was in exile, some years before the drafting of the *Code civil*, he wrote another important work, published posthumously in 1820, entitled *De l'usage et l'abus de l'esprit philosophique durant le XVIIIe*, which demonstrates his wide reading and the influence of the intellectual contacts he made in Germany. After analysing its causes he saw the Revolution as a 'sort of war of all against all' which stirred up the 'dregs of the nation' and produced numerous 'bloody tribunals' more 'awful' than invasion by barbarians. For him 1789 marked the triumph of 'false doctrines dressed up as a solemn declaration of rights', indeed he attributed the Revolution to the passion for systematisation, and deplored the part played by the *philosophes* and the *Encyclopédie*, the birth of 'public opinion' and the concomitant decline in public morals. Portalis counters these false doctrines with his own opinions, hoping thereby to refute Rousseau: with no belief in an 'absolute state of nature', as distinct from society which is a fact and not a contract, he places a high value on the family, 'the first and most natural of societies' as he says (actually echoing Rousseau ...), in which the husband has the power to direct the domestic partnership, and the father has power over the children, though limited in time. Portalis rejects the idea of perfect equality and defends distinctions of wealth and variety of professions. What really counts for him is moral duty which he derives from feeling and instinct, rejecting both the philosophy of Kant and the utilitarian theories of 'interest properly understood'.

In many respects Portalis's thinking, counter-revolutionary and idealist, is akin to that of Herder and Burke, both of whom he regarded highly, and even of Bonald and Montlosier, who might seem to be opponents in the 'apparent dispute' over the *Code civil*. Portalis also knew and profited from the works of Mandeville, Smith and Ferguson, and drew on Locke and Montesquieu, so it is not surprising that his analysis of the causes of the Revolution was to be largely taken up by Tocqueville. Indeed, in stating that 'overgovernment is bad government' Portalis is not very far from the liberalism then beginning to surface.

B. Counter-revolution and liberalism

Others among the codifiers were also influenced by both counter-revolutionary authors and the 'fathers' of liberalism, for at the time these two emergent schools of thought were not yet wholly divergent. Indeed when the Code was being produced neither the idea of 'liberalism' nor even the very word was yet current, and the intellectual relations between writers recently dead such as Adam Smith (†1790) and Edmund Burke (†1797) and contemporaries like Bentham, Jean-Baptiste Say and Benjamin Constant were complex. This conjuncture explains how one can find in a lawyer like Maleville both reactionary sentiments, as on divorce, and observations redolent of liberalism such as 'Government is best when it can achieve its aim by roundabout methods and seems to be governing the least.'

It is not easy to ascertain how well the codifiers knew the works of Smith, Say (whose *Traité d'économie politique* appeared in 1803) or Bentham (whose *Traité de législation civile et pénale* was published in Paris in French in 1802), but there are surprising echoes of these authors in their reasoning on the way the legislator should use the vices and virtues of the citizen, the importance of utility and the need to reconstruct the bonds of society. When people under the Consulate and the Empire observed that some of the ideas in the *Code civil* were 'liberal' they were not entirely wrong.

III. Beyond ideologies

Not all the rules in the *Code civil* can be explained by the value-judgements of the codifiers, for in addition to their views about the nature of man and the organisation of society one must take into account the rise of the Napoleonic state with its taste for ambiguity (A) and the inherited culture of lawyers which is so resistant to fashions in thinking (B).

A. A State without principles?

The regime of the Consulate and the Empire, with its numerous dictatorial characteristics, was marked by a 'withering away of ideologies'. As Louis Bergeron wrote, it was 'short of roots, principles and legitimation'. Napoleon's aim, as his speech at his coronation in 1804 makes clear, was to reconcile his own increasingly monarchical power with the maintenance of the 'social achievements' of the Revolution, but the role of law is always ambivalent when politics operate behind a façade of constitutionalism. Under cover of appeal to law and even the idea of equality public liberties can be restricted, new hierarchies created and different classes of citizen treated differently. Bonaparte knew how to conscript both law and the ideologies fashionable at the time of the Consulate in furtherance of his plan to increase the prerogatives of the state, the big winner under codification. The authoritarian view of social integration, like the concession of a 'quasi-judicial role' to the paterfamilias, eventually benefits a state armed with several devices which enable it to impose its authority in an unobvious way. The rules of the *Code civil* helped to increase the control of the state over certain kinds of property, such as mines and marshes, and over certain transactions, such as loan of money and hire of services, a control which increased from 1800 to 1814 in the Consulate and the Empire. By disguising this takeover of the private sphere by the state the Code may have enabled itself both to survive through a dirigiste regime and then to adapt itself to a polity more honestly liberal.

B. The survival of lawyerly tradition

The *Code civil*, as Bentham noted, was drafted by lawyers of the 'old school', trained in pre-Revolutionary law. It is therefore instinct with the professionalism of the traditional lawyer. The lawyerly tradition in France was much influenced by Jansenism, exemplified by Domat and Pothier, and its specific sense of social relations, justice and order can be detected in the codal provisions such as those on proper conduct and good faith. The doctrine on which the *Code civil* drew was thus largely pre-Revolutionary even if the Revolution itself was its immediate political stimulus, and the way it combined this age-old lawyerly morality, often pessimistic and antirationalist, with the ideas fashionable at the time of the Consulate may explain the richness of the text and the 'flexibility' for which it is famous.

Section 3: The sociology of the Code

To inquire into the sociology of the *Code civil* means asking how the codifiers viewed the society of their day and what effect the Code had on social developments in the nineteenth century. It is clear that the predominance of ownership in the *Code Napoléon* reflects the pre-eminence of the notables so prominent in the Napoleonic period and throughout most of the century (I), but it is more difficult to determine the role accorded by the *Code civil* to commerce and industry or the working class, since it does not deal explicitly with either business or labour (II).

I. A Code designed for notables

Historians are increasingly reluctant to decry the *Code Napoléon* as a 'bourgeois' code, seeing how difficult it is to decide who, or how important, the 'bourgeois' were in 1804. In Napoleon's day the term 'notables' was used to denote all property owners whose wealth, taxability and electoral power gave them a say in society, whether they were noble or commoner, urban or rural. The importance of landed proprietors was recognised by the codifiers (A) and they were much concerned with the question of dividing up their estates (B).

A. The power of landowners

The draftsmen of the *Code civil* constantly emphasised the economic and social importance of land ownership, 'free and productive land' being the only guarantee of lasting wealth (Treihard). According to Bonaparte, property owners, especially the notables whose property was taxable, were 'the most reliable support for the security and peace of states'. Jaubert, the tribune, went even further in stating '[O]ur political system is based primarily on landed property'.

Like the French economists of the eighteenth century the draftsmen believed agriculture to be the 'real source of human nourishment' and that agricultural productivity would be best increased by leaving individuals 'free to cultivate' their own land: as Portalis said, 'personal interest will ensure energetic and careful husbandry'. Following the physiocrats' belief in giving landowners their freedom, the *Code civil* permitted enclosure, diminished common pastureland and supported the landowner in disputes with the tenant farmer or sharecropper. A lease of rural land could be made orally, it could be short, and could be terminated easily; furthermore, the collection of rents was facilitated by provisions which protected the owner from the 'faithlessness' of the farmer, to the extent of allowing imprisonment for non-payment. The farmer was admittedly protected if the land were sold, but the security of his tenure was justified by the general interest in the improvement of the land. The Code was determinedly in favour of agricultural 'capitalism'.

B. The division of estates

The codifiers recognised that the distribution of wealth would inevitably be unequal, and that this could well be used for purposes of social engineering. As Portalis saw, '[I]t is an error to suppose that wealth and social differences lead to abuse'. At the same time 'the splendour of the great families' and the fact that it had been possible for landed capital to be immobilised for generations to the advantage of a single individual were anathema to the old revolutionaries who witnessed the return of many of the *émigrés* and the re-establishment of the wealth of the nobility. Some of this anti-aristocratic feeling still existed in 1804 and expressed itself in hostility towards primogeniture and entails.

The views of Le Play might lead one to believe that the codifiers were uninterested in the economic effects of the rules of succession, but in fact they were just as concerned as their revolutionary predecessors. Bonaparte was particularly worried abut the risk of 'undue division of modest fortunes', and viewed with dismay the 'selling up of the family home', the 'heart' of family solidarity. Bigot de Préameneu also warned his colleagues about dividing land up so much that the 'small estate' would disappear. Some of those who drafted the Code, including Berlier and Réal, did favour the division of estates, and thought they had found a middle way by increasing the amount of which the testator could freely dispose and in permitting ascendants to divide their property inter vivos; they cannot be blamed for the movement towards equality of treatment and birth control which was underway before drafting even started. In fact fathers during the nineteenth century very rarely used their remaining freedom of disposition so as to favour one of their children over the others: the subdivision of land was due to the preferences of the French citizenry rather than the provisions of the *Code civil*.

II. A Code for social change?

Even if they could not predict the importance of the forthcoming industrial 'revolution' the draftsmen of the *Code civil* were perfectly aware of the economic changes which had already occurred. There are frequent references in the *travaux préparatoires* to the fact that commerce had become 'the main source of public wealth' (Grenier). The society envisaged by the Code is far from being dominated by *rentiers* (note Bonaparte's hostility to rent charges which could not be commuted). It was to be based on work and industry in the old sense: property must be productive, the spendthrift disapproved of because he neither works nor saves. Yet at the same time one notes unease at the 'speculations of international commerce' (Leroy) and the possible demands of the 'working class'. Thus the new law tried to reconcile two principles of social control: making business active while keeping it clean (A) and restraining the 'proletarians' (B).

A. Facilitating fair trading

Although the contrary has long been believed, the codifiers were very far from neglecting the importance of movable property. Treilhard noted, admittedly with some regret, that 'there has been a considerable increase in the movable wealth of the citizen' and that 'land perhaps does not account for one-half of their assets'. Portalis realised that 'wealth in movables comes from commerce' and that the people who had most of their assets in that form would be the richest in the world. The absence of any particular protection for movables in the Code may thus be seen as designed to facilitate competition and the 'circulation of capital', which is frequently mentioned in the *travaux préparatoires*. Nor can one infer from the fact that the Code contains no specific and explicit provisions about them that the codifiers failed to realise the importance of companies or the idea of the 'legal person' (*personne morale*) or the enterprise as such, which figures only in the rules relating to the transmission of a manufacturing firm to a person adopted.

But this must be seen in context. The reason why most questions of commerce were merely adumbrated in the *Code civil* is that there was soon to be a Code of Commerce (realised in 1807 by another 'team' of draftsmen). Again, the codifiers sometimes expressed suspicion of certain commercial activities. A sale of land could be rescinded for lesion in order to 'punish excessive greed at the expense of another', the government was given power to limit the rate of interest so that a distinction could be drawn between 'businessmen' and 'manufacturers' who need cheap credit, and the idle 'capitalists' (to use Maleville's expression); and disapproval of life assurance was presented as a way of thwarting 'the vulgar commercial spirit'. In this way memories of the 'speculators' under the Directory and the moralist detestation of 'insatiable greed for money' helped to continue the tradition of *dirigisme*, which still had a lively future.

B. Containing the proletariat

Although the codifiers occasionally spoke of 'factories' and sometimes of more modest 'workshops', they probably had no idea of the future growth in the number of the workforce. They were of course aware that in town and country there were huge numbers of 'workers' who had no property at all and had to work for the 'affluent' (Mouricault and Jaubert). Peasants, domestic servants and handymen had to have work and wages, and so we have the various forms of contract of service and the justification for the privilege over movables given to 'servants' (Art 2101, 4°). As is shown by the article which directs the children of adulterous or incestuous relationships to the 'mechanical arts' (Art 764), manual labour was reserved for the very poorest: there was no question of 'liberal arts' or intellectual property. So, too, the statutory regime of community property in marriage is addressed to those 'whose only wealth is in the children and their labour' (Duveyrier), those marriages without property where the woman works at the 'meanest occupations'. Finally, there remains something of the revolutionary dream of becoming a nation of property owners, for then there would be fewer mere labourers: by dividing up estates on death, according to Réal, one can 'reduce the size of the proletarian class'.

But, as was said in connection with peasant farmers, the codifiers were alert to see that the labouring classes might be dangerous. They may 'state yet again the principle of individual liberty' as regards the hiring of domestic servants and other workers (characteristically amalgamated as 'those who work'), but they placed more faith in the 'master', and if Art 1781 is virtually the only article in the *Code civil* which bespeaks inequality in the classes of society, this is really because the control of the working classes was essentially a matter for the police and was regulated by other texts, such as the Law of 12 April 1803. It remains true that in admitting the existence of a class of workers without according them any particular place (unlike the Prussian Code which subdivided the citizenry) the *Code Napoléon* was once again relatively open to future social developments.

Chapter 6: The Code at Home and Abroad

The *Code civil* has pride of place among the Napoleonic codes not only by reason of its contents and originality but also because of its longevity and geographical spread. Its structure and most of its articles (over 1,200 out of 2,281) are today just as they were on the date of promulgation, yet the *Code civil*, modified but not replaced, is still basic to the private law of France despite the enormous growth in collateral legislation and divergent case-law (I). It has also spread throughout the world, whether by force of arms or by its own magnetism, though with the passing of time it has been affected in different ways in the countries which adopted it (II).

Section I: From the *Code Napoléon* to the Code of today

The first partial modification of the *Code civil* occurred in 1807, the year in which it was officially designated the *Code Napoléon*. There then ensued, under successive political regimes, a long series of transformations which resulted in the text with which the Code is poised to enter the twenty-first century. In this development the 1880s constitute a watershed; that was when republicans achieved a majority in the legislature and new generations of lawyers were less ready to treat the text of the Code of 1804 as immutable. The precise turning-point could be located in 1884, when divorce was reintroduced. This rather surprisingly triggered a series of reforms of family law, taking it away from the lines chosen in 1804, just as laws legitimating trades unions mark a development of labour relations very far from the ideas of the Consulate. For the first time in 80 years, the *Code civil* began to be seriously questioned (I). Nevertheless it is by no means obsolete, for in the nineteenth and twentieth centuries French private law developed in line with the slogan of Saleilles (*agrégé* in 1884) '[B]eyond the *Code civil* by means of the *Code civil*' (II).

I. Eight decades of dominance

Between 1804 and 1884 the *Code civil* was subjected to very few attacks: its domination of the whole of French private law was almost absolute.

Constitutions may have played musical chairs between the First Empire and the Third Republic, but the *Code civil* remained in place, with little legislation on private law (A). The respect accorded to the Code by writers (B) and courts (C) may be explained by the conservatism of lawyers drawn from the ranks of the notables who were content with a text which satisfied the growing bourgeoisie. Resistance to the Code in the provinces was very slight, which shows that national unity was winning out over local diversity (D).

A. The restraint of the legislature

The draftsmen of the *Code civil* may have regarded it as 'the ark of the covenant', but they still envisaged that it could be modified in detail. Thus the Law of 3 September 1807, which changed its name from the *Code civil des Français* to the *Code Napoléon*, also introduced a number of 'corrections' (Bigot de Préameneu) in the law of succession (Art 896) after the creation of *majorats* (see below p. 107). If Napoleon I had no intention of making any further changes in his Code, the attitude of Louis XVIII is more surprising: although he regarded the Code as 'disgraced by the name of Napoléon' and therefore reinstated the title of *Code civil*, he saw nothing more in it than 'a collection of the prior ordinances and customs of the realm'. In his Charter he therefore undertook to maintain it in force, while leaving the door open for legislative changes, especially where 'religious doctrine' was involved. Shortly afterwards the Law of 8 May 1816 abrogated the provisions of the Code on divorce, and then in 1819 the Law of 14 July abolished Art 912 which had limited the succession rights of foreigners. These 'amputations' had the support of Maleville, one of the original draftsmen, and were consistent with opinions current under the Consulate. Proposals from 'reactionaries' were unsuccessful: Parliament refused to return the register of civil status to the keeping of the Church and in 1826 the peers themselves killed a bill which would have permitted a form of primogeniture.

The July monarchy (1830–48) altered only two articles of the *Code civil* (164 and 896, on marriage with a parent's sibling and substitutions respectively), and the Second Republic (1848–52) only six others (abolition of *majorats* in 1849, and reforms on the detail of the publication of marriage contracts and the denial of paternity in 1850), but more changes were made in the Second Empire (1852–70), under which the Code regained its title as *Code Napoléon*. The articles on civil death, imprisonment of debtors and disputes between master and servant (the unequal Art 1781) were abrogated in 1854, 1867 and 1868 respectively, and a Law of 23 March 1855 introduced registration of title to land – a delayed response to those who had long criticised the Code for keeping land-holdings secret. These changes, which bespeak a degree of economic and social liberalism, left the provisions on the family and property untouched.

B. The deference of scholars

Because he distrusted the way lawyers might interpret his Code, Napoleon did his best to subject legal education to strict control by the state. From the Law of 13 March 1804 (22 *ventôse* year XII) until 1875 only the *Écoles*, subsequently *Facultés*, could teach French law, essentially private law, that is the *Code civil*. The three-year programme of the *licence en droit*, designed to train practitioners, consisted predominantly of courses on the Code of Napoleon. Furthermore, the method of instruction, by dictation, was fixed by directives from the ministry and the professors were strictly supervised until the end of the Second Empire. It is therefore not surprising that those who wrote about the law, increasingly within the universities, were imbued with respect for the letter of the *Code civil*, if not its spirit.

Most of those who delivered courses and wrote commentaries and treatises followed the order of the Code article by article, and tended to assert that they were only laying out the positive law in an exegetical manner – such was the effect of the cult of law and the admiration for the Code – but while it is true that most of the writers on private law kept their eyes on the *Code civil* and moderated their criticisms out of intellectual and social conformism, it is actually inaccurate to speak of a School of Exegesis, since every author had a way of trotting out theories of his own which had no real basis in the text of the Code.

C. The daring of the courts

Under the First Empire the courts were constrained to apply the *Code civil* strictly: they had to give reasons for their judgments, could not make decisions of general application (Art 5), were supervised by the *Cour de cassation*, and were subject to a reference to the Head of State in the event of divergent interpretations (Law of 16 September 1807). The situation became somewhat more flexible when the powers of the Court of Cassation were increased under the Law of 1 April 1837, and the benefits of case law came to be more widely recognised in accordance with the ideas put forward by Portalis in his *Discours préliminaire*.

It is true that to begin with the courts often applied the *Code civil* in a 'mechanical' manner, but even well before the 1880s they can be seen to have taken certain liberties with the text. At the outset the judges, who hardly ever had recourse to the *travaux préparatoires*, were more familiar with prior law than with the novel doctrine of the Code, and quite readily cited bits of Roman law and the customs. They were thus led to interpret certain terms of the Code, such as *faute, injure* and *erreur*, and fill gaps (could one adopt one's own illegitimate child?), and apply texts in an unliteral manner, as on the implied agency of the wife and the alienability of movables within the dowry. In addition to such decisions *praeter legem* decisions can be found which rather conflict with principles contained in the Code: for example, notwithstanding the prohibition on paternity suits, the courts upheld claims for damages against the seducer. Sometimes their decisions went clearly *contra legem*. It is evident, for example, that the lower courts (from 1830) and the *Cour de cassation* (in 1867) violated the terms of Art 331 of the *Code civil* when they permitted parents guilty of incest to legitimate the child if they had obtained a *dispense de mariage*. More research certainly needs to be done into the judicial archives, especially the records of judges of the peace and tribunals of first instance, before we can say how frequently such apparently bold decisions were made (often out of deference to prior law), but by and large it is safe to say that in the nineteenth century the 'judges and notables' showed little sign of any wish to throw doubt on the foundations of the *Code civil*.

D. The resistance of the localities

We do not yet know enough about actual practice in the nineteenth century to say to what extent the *Code civil* was really applied. Since it represented the desires of the notables, it was unlikely to be rejected by property owners and wealthy fathers, but was it used by the lower classes whose lack of means prevented their engaging in expensive procedures to vindicate their rights? Even if labour relations were barely covered by the flexible rules of the *Code civil*, the law surely applied to the family life of peasants and workmen (for poor people in the countryside clearly did get married); indeed, after the introduction of legal aid in 1851, an increasing number of claims for judicial separation were made by claimants in very modest circumstances.

But there is evidence that the *Code civil* was sometimes ignored in the provinces, and that there were survivals from prior law which only fell away after quite a long period of transition. Thus in several regions inferior property rights which had not been abolished along with feudalism continued to survive, such as emphyteusis, *bail à comptant* or terminable ownership (*domaine congéable*). In parts of the south of France and Normandy spouses continued for a while to retain the dowry system, while in the north one finds marriage contracts with provisions reminiscent of the customs (which could not be referred to by name, Art 1390 *Code civil*). People were perfectly free to contract in this way, but owners of property did occasionally resort to fraudulent devices in order to favour the eldest son and to avoid the rules limiting the amount of property of which they were free to dispose. Further evidence of islands of resistance to the Code may be found in the tendency of several jurisdictions in the south to refuse to follow the views of the *Cour de cassation* on the right of ascendants to provide for their descendants (*partage d'ascendants*).

II. Beyond the Code civil *by means of the* Code civil

After the 1880s the *Code civil* (which effectively lost its name of *Code Napoléon* after the collapse of the Second Empire) came under more frequent attack. Legislative reforms took place both inside and outside the Code (A). A number of writers favoured complete revision of the Code, and though this never happened, they had an influence, especially on the extensive modification of Book One from the 1960s onwards (B). In view of the vast amount of case-law and the proliferation of new branches of law one is led to ask whether the *Code civil* is still significant today. Is it simply a compilation which has had its day (C) or does it still represent the heartland of French private law (D)?

A. *From reform to decodification*

The Law of 27 July 1884 which reintroduced divorce might be thought to represent a return to the original *Code civil*, the closure of a detour opened in 1816, but this is not quite so: the Law was not as radical as the *Code civil*, in that it still rejected divorce by mutual consent, but it went much beyond it in abandoning the differential treatment of man and wife as regards adultery. It thus started a movement for the reform of family law which continued, with stops and starts, throughout the Third Republic. The principal steps in the reform of core articles of the *Code civil* are the Law of 25 March 1896 on the inheritance rights of natural children, those of 20 June 1896 and 21 June 1907 on marriage, the law of 16 November 1912 on paternity claims, the Law of 19 June 1923 permitting the adoption of minors, the decree-law of 30 October 1935 on the father's disciplinary powers and the Law of 18 February 1938 abolishing the husband's power.

Some important reforms of private law took place outside the *Code civil*. The Law of 24 July 1889, weakening paternal power, was not included in the Code, perhaps because of its connection with criminal law, nor was the Law of 13 July 1907 on the right of married women to dispose of their earnings as they wished, though this was inconsistent with the matrimonial regimes then in force. The very important law on industrial accidents of 9 April 1898 affected only one article of the *Code civil* (on priorities) while the decree-law of 29 July 1939 – significantly called the *Code de la famille* by practitioners – was only partially integrated. The reforms of the Third Republic (1873–1940) on the law of the countryside, labour law and the special contracts were carried out by means of special legislation which barely affected the provisions of the *Code civil* on property and contract. From then on an increasing quantity of private law was to be found outside the *Code civil*, as is shown by the numerous articles which have lost their text and retained only their number (Arts 12 and 13, 17–21, 381, 773 etc.).

B. Revision or replacement?

At the beginning of the twentieth century many jurists, struck by the proliferation of new laws and the growth of case law, especially as regards unjust enrichment and liability for damage done by things, came to regard the Code as obsolete. Larnaud, for example, felt that he was able to write '[W]e no longer have a Civil Code'. The question of *révision* (rather an equivocal term in this context) was raised by the *Société d'études législatives*, founded in 1901, and it was directly addressed at the time of the Code's centenary. Some lawyers were opposed to any major modification of the code, while the 'reformers' were divided between those who favoured a simple reconstruction and those who wanted a code entirely new. In December 1904 the Minister of Justice set up a huge extra-Parliamentary Commission of 61 members, including politicians, legal professionals and men of letters. There were several working sessions, one of which generated the suggestion that man and wife should be obliged to *love* each other, but no concrete proposal was ever made, and Parliament preferred to continue with sporadic and partial reforms. The attempt to produce a revision of the *Code civil* had too many adversaries in the world of politics and law, and its final defeat was shown by the production in 1910 of a *Code de Travail*, though this was a mere compilation of laws already in existence.

Recension returned to the order of the day after the Liberation. In June 1945 the government set up a commission of reform with 12 members, all jurists, under the presidency of Léon Julliot de La Morandière. It was to study the possibility of replacing the Code with an entirely new text, taking account of the way society had evolved since 1804. In 1953 it produced a preliminary book and Book One on persons and family, followed in 1962 by another on rights of succession, but again no text was submitted to Parliament, and when the reformist enthusiasm of the Liberation had died down, the jurists were more than ever divided on the question how far the changes should go, and the politicians of the Fourth Republic had other fish to fry.

Subsequently, however, the Code has been rejuvenated, owing principally to the efforts of Dean Carbonnier. From 1964 to 1975 laws were passed on family law which altered whole titles of the *Code civil* (guardianship, matrimonial regimes, adoption, adults without capacity, parental authority, paternity and divorce). The plan of the Code and the numbering of its articles were retained as far as possible, a technique of grafting which sought to reconcile the retention of the formal structure with a major transformation of its substance. It has since been applied to certain areas of the law of obligations (such as partnership in 1978) and spasmodically in more recent reforms on the law relating to respect for the human body (1985, 1987, 1993 and 1994), adoption (1996), the civil solidarity pact (*Pacs*; in 1999), compensation on divorce (2000), succession law (2001), the family name (2002) and the prohibition of reproductive cloning (2003).

C. Is the Code obsolete?

The accelerated amendment of the *Code civil* during the past 30 years has defused any major movement towards decodification, but has it stopped the decline of a text which is still largely that of 1804? The technique of bringing the code up to date by minor amendments, which has accelerated since 1985, runs the risk of reducing it to a congeries of rules which are heterogeneous in date, spirit and coverage rather than being connected and ordered as they were in 1804. The Code might even be said to be almost monstrous, given such excrescences as Arts 311–320 or 832–834, vacant spaces and parts which are really moribund. Such coherence as remained has been further diminished by the introduction of the novel civil solidarity pact, wholly at odds with the civilian tradition which underlay previous reforms.

Again, more and more legislation in private law has taken place outside the Code, such as the Law of 10 July 1965 on co-ownership, the Law of 5 July 1985 on traffic accidents, and the rash of laws on residential leases. Indeed, this spate of legislation has given birth to new 'codes', though they are really no more than compilations: the *Code rural* (1955), the *Code des Assurances* (1976), the *Code de la construction et de l'habitation* (1978), the *Code de la propriété intellectuelle* (1992), and the *Code de la consommation* (1993). Even if we leave aside commercial and labour law, the *Code civil* can no longer claim to comprise the great bulk of private law as it did in the nineteenth century.

Finally, private law is now informed from different sources: constitutional law has had an increasing impact, especially when the 'fundamental nature of the right of ownership' was recognised as a constitutional value in 1992, as have public international law (such as the Vienna *Convention* on the International Sale of Goods (CISG) and the New York *Convention* of the Rights of the Child), and above all European Community Law (the direct effect of treaties, regulations and some directives). To these we must add the growing amount of law created by the courts.

D. The heart still beats

But the *Code civil* has survived all this, thanks to its solidity and flexibility. The legislator has recently testified to its belief in its symbolic value by revitalising Title I of Book One, now entitled 'civil rights'. Indeed the *Code civil* can be said to have regained its role as the basic text for the whole of private law with the insertion of Art 9 on the right to respect for one's private life (1970), Art 10 on the duty to assist the courts (1972), Art 16 on the rules governing respect for the human body (1994), and the reintroduction in Arts 17–33 (1993) of the main principles of the law of nationality, which had disappeared from the *Code civil* in 1927.

The introduction of the civil solidarity pact in deference to those who demanded it and the acceptance of the evidential value of electronic signatures in 2000 show how open to modernisation the Code has been. The number of grafts has increased, but the trunk has retained its vitality, and the courts still resolve novel disputes in private law, even in commercial and labour law, by reference to the most general codal articles (Arts 544, 1129, 1134, 1371, 1382 and 1384).

Section 2: The *Code civil* abroad

French lawyers are apt to exaggerate the influence of the *Code civil* abroad, and to misunderstand the reasons for it. It was mainly by force of arms that the Code was introduced in Europe in Napoleon's time (I). After 1814 the main reason for its retention was its 'revolutionary prestige' (II), and during the nineteenth century, and to a lesser extent in the twentieth, it was treated as a model because of its intrinsic qualities (III).

I. Expansion through imperialism

Napoleon was sure that his *Code civil*, if not 'perfect', was the 'code of the century' and wanted it to be adopted as widely as possible. Not only was it brought into force in the *Grand Empire* (A) but severe pressure was brought on subservient states and allies to adopt it so that the Code could become, as Bigot de Préameneu put it, 'the common law of Europe' (B).

A. In the Grand Empire

When the *Code civil* was promulgated in 1804 the following were departments of France: Belgium and Luxembourg (from 1795), four departments on the Rhine (from 1800), the department of Léman, including Geneva (from 1798), and six departments in the Piedmont (from 1802, down to five in 1805). In all these the *Code civil* applied automatically, like all other French laws. In the Belgian department and those on the left bank of the Rhine French law had already abolished feudalism and introduced civil marriage and divorce, so the publication of the *Code civil*, in French, was not much of a shock and quite popular.

In the departments created after 1804 the situation was rather different: these included three departments in what had been the Republic of Genoa (1805), four out of Tuscany and Parma (1808), two around Rome (1810), 13 out of Holland, the Hanseatic cities and various German principalities (such as the Duchy of Arenberg), and finally the Valais in Switzerland (1810). In these places the introduction of French law, including a partial abolition of feudalism resulting from the laws of the *Assemblée Constituante*, was a brutal innovation. It could even frustrate existing plans for codification. It did so in Holland, where a civil code, described as a 'French bonbonnière full of Dutch pralines', had been published, quite close to the French model but containing some fairly significant deviations (as on matrimonial regimes and real rights resulting from feudalism). This attempt to adapt the *Code civil français* was swept aside in 1811 when French law and language were imposed by Napoleon I, who four years earlier had told the King, his brother, to bring in 'his' Code. Much the same happened in the former Duchy of Arenberg where a slightly modified *Code Napoléon* was introduced in 1808–09.

B. *In satellite states*

Since Napoleon had made himself King of Italy the introduction of the *Code civil* there was swift. Much to the displeasure of Italian jurists hostile to divorce and the statutory matrimonial regime, an official Italian translation was promulgated in 1806, thwarting previous efforts at codification in the Cisalpine Republic. The Code was applied in Lombardy-Venetia, Modena and the Marche, as well as the Illyrian provinces, and while people there were uneasy about the family law emanating from France they were quite favourable to the new property regime.

In the Kingdom of Naples matters were more complicated. In June 1806 Napoleon firmly advised his brother Joseph to bring in the *Code civil*: 'Then everything you dislike will shortly disappear, and everything you want to keep will be confirmed.' At the time the emperor was ready to accept that divorce not be introduced, but by 1808 he regarded divorce as essential to the code, so he refused to allow Murat, who had become King of Naples, to effect any modifications. The whole Code was therefore translated and applied from 1809 onwards in the south of Italy, with the exception of Sicily which was not under French domination. As it turned out, divorce was barely used and there was opposition to the new system of land ownership.

To the German states of the Rheinish Confederation, which were under Napoleon's protection, it was gently suggested by word of mouth that the *Code civil* be adopted. This occurred mostly in the places nearest France. Jérôme Bonaparte, as King of Westphalia, had a translation of the Code Napoleon brought into force there in 1808, though the church was allowed to retain the register of civil status and some feudal charges were left in place untill commuted, to the irritation of the peasantry. In the Grand Duchy of Berg the Code was introduced in 1809–10, the surviving feudal charges being subject to commutation. The Grand Duchy of Baden followed a more independent path and published its *Badische Landrecht* in 1809, a version of the Code Napoleon with annotations which presaged modifications (such as a much greater facility for bringing paternity suits). In Frankfurt, the Code Napoleon was in force after 1811 but with numerous exceptions (divorce was unavailable to Catholics). Short-lived projects for adapting the code to Bavaria (1808–10), Anhalt, Hesse and Nassau were adjourned, and much of Germany (Saxony and, of course, Prussia) remained opposed to the Code Napoleon despite the interest in it shown by many local jurists.

In the Grand Duchy of Warsaw, created in 1807 with a new constitution, the Code Napoleon was introduced in 1808. The official French version (the Polish translation being quite unofficial) met with serious opposition, for although the nobility retained control of their land, they were afraid of the effect of the abolition of serfdom and preferred the Prussian system of land registration to the French system of mortgages. Finally, the clergy, who retained their control of the register of civil status except in Warsaw, succeeded quite well in thwarting the introduction of civil marriage and divorce.

II. The Code retained

After the fall of Napoleon in 1814 a vengeful spirit of nationalism and reaction led to the abrogation of the *Code civil* in many European countries, but as it was still associated with the ideas of the Revolution, especially as regards the ending of feudalism, it was kept in force in several areas as an example of modern legislation and enjoyed much popular support. 'Provisional' retention sometimes lasted for decades, as it did in Geneva from 1816 to 1912. The retention was prolonged in important areas such as Belgium (A), Poland (B), the Rhineland (C) and Italy (D), which call for special attention.

A. The Netherlands and Belgium

In 1814–15 Belgium and the former United Provinces were regrouped into the Kingdom of the Netherlands. A commission charged with codification was set up under the new constitution, but its draft of a civil code ran into serious opposition, especially in the Belgian provinces. In 1826 a compromise was reached and another code, quite like the Code Napoleon in substance, was to come into force in 1831. A revolution in Belgium in the summer of 1830 frustrated these plans, and the provisional Belgian government immediately revoked the ordinance promulgating the Netherlands civil code. The liberal reaction triggered a movement in favour of French law, and though the constitution allowed for a revision of the projected civil code, it was in fact the *Code Napoléon* itself which was brought into force after 1831. Although a fair number of statutory modifications have taken place since then – one on privileges and mortgages in 1851, one on paternity suits in 1908, and laws abolishing the married woman's incapacity in 1932 and 1958 – one can truly say that Belgium has been even more faithful than France to the text of 1804 (for example, the rules of divorce which were abrogated or modified in France have been kept in force).

In the Netherlands, by contrast, nationalist feeling led to the adoption of a new code in 1838. Notwithstanding the desire expressed that it distance itself from the French model, many of the articles of this code, which remained in force until 1982, echo those of the *Code Napoléon*. In Luxembourg the *Code Napoléon* remained in force after 1814 and suffered no significant modifications until the twentieth century.

B. Poland – a special case

The Kingdom of Poland was established by the Congress of Vienna, to be ruled by the Tsar of Russia under a constitution which retained existing law. The *Code Napoléon* was therefore kept in force, though with important alterations as regards mortgages (1818) and especially marriage (in 1836 marriage again became a matter for the Church and divorce was suppressed). The Polish nobility was not keen on it, but popular feeling throughout the nineteenth century regarded the French code as a token of independence from Russia and defended it, translated and applied in Russian though it was. It was maintained in central Poland when that country was reconstituted in 1918, but in 1933 a new Code of Obligations was introduced and the *Code Napoléon* was abrogated in late 1946.

C. The Rhinelands

When Napoleon fell the *Code civil* was abrogated in Westphalia, which reverted to Hanover, but it was maintained in Oldenburg, the Grand Duchy of Baden (in the local form) and the Bavarian Palatinate. It was also retained in the previously French departments on the left bank of the Rhine and the parts of what had been the Grand Duchy of Berg until 1814, when they were annexed by Prussia. Attempts to introduce the Prussian Code in the Rhinelands in the first half of the nineteenth century were thwarted by local assemblies, for the powerful bourgeoisie and even some of the nobles there remained attached to the French code, which accordingly remained in force, with a special chamber in the *Reichsgericht* for appeals on French law, until 1900 when the BGB was promulgated.

D. Italy

The *Code Napoléon* was abrogated in most of the Italian states in 1814–15. It was replaced in Lombardy-Venice, except as to mortgages, by the Austrian ABGB of 1811, and in the Piedmont, where the prior law was re-established. It was also replaced in the Papal States, in Modena and in Tuscany. In Naples divorce was suppressed in 1815, the law of succession reformed in 1816 and a new code adopted in 1819. The Code remained in force rather longer in Parma and Piacenza until 1820, while Marie-Louise was in charge, and in Genoa, whose territory became part of Piedmont but not subject to Piedmontese law until 1837. Lucca is an exceptional case, for the *Code Napoléon* remained in force there until the Italian *Codice civile* was promulgated in 1866, subject to the excision of the provisions on civil marriage and divorce which were incompatible with current policies in the Italian states.

Although there was some opposition to the *Code Napoléon*, especially in Tuscany, it continued to have a significant influence on the law in Italy throughout the nineteenth century. First, the codes adopted in several of the states were more or less inspired by the *Code civil*. Thus the private law of the Kingdom of the Two Sicilies (1819) is very close to the *Code Napoléon* both in structure and content, apart from marriage, which became exclusively a matter for the church. Likewise in Parma with its civil code of 1820, and to a lesser extent in the Piedmont where the *Codice civile Albertino* of 1837 was rather more conservative as regards paternal power, successions and, of course, marriage. Again, the principle of equality which runs through the French *Code civil* made it a rallying point for liberals and those fighting for unification, to the point where in 1859 the deputy from Tuscany, Montanelli, cried out: 'Long live the Kingdom of Italy, long live King Victor-Emmanuele, and long live the

Code Napoléon!' When Italy was unified the Code Napoleon was introduced into the areas incorporated into the Piedmont in 1859 (the Legations – Bologna, Ferrara, Ravenna and Forli) until the infant kingdom produced its own civil code in 1865. The *Codice civile* bears many of the marks of its French elder brother (civil marriage admitted, though divorce excluded). The *Code Napoléon* had graduated from a symbol to a model.

III. The Code as model

During the nineteenth and twentieth centuries the *Code civil* of France boosted the codification movement in European countries where it had never been brought into force (A). It also had a remarkable influence in the New World (B) where the nascent states saw the text as liberal and modern. The influence of the *Code Napoléon* in Asia and Africa must be seen in the context of other European models and the process of colonialisation (C).

A. Codification in Europe

During the nineteenth century states which wished to codify their private law looked much more to the *Code Napoléon* than to the Codes of Prussia or Austria, and followed the structure and rules of the French code because of its 'liberal' and reassuring image, the clarity of its language – the French language had great prestige at the time – and its technical merits, enhanced by the writings of French scholars, readily available in translation. The Italian *Codice civile* of 1865, which remained in force until 1942, is one of the best examples of adaptation, accepting improvements made after 1804 (as for the system of mortgages) and deferring to local policy, as by declining to adopt divorce or the statutory regime for matrimonial property. The Portuguese Civil Code of 1867 also shows the influence of Napoleon's legislation, despite its adoption of a different structure and refusal to accept divorce. Roumania is an even stronger case, for two-thirds of the articles in the Civil Code, adopted under Prince Alexander Ian Cuza shortly after the unification of Roumania of 1864, are taken from the *Code Napoléon*. For a long time it was thought to have been rejected because the peasant majority disliked the division of estates, but now it can be seen as a stage in developing and modernising the law prior to 1918, for example by the introduction of civil marriage. In Spain the experience of Napoleon's troops had rather sullied the image of his Code, but even so the *Código civil* of 1889 borrowed many its features, more than 250 of its articles, such as Art 213, being adopted virtually verbatim. Marriage, however, remained under the control of the church and was indissoluble. With the promulgation of the German Civil Code (BGB) in 1900 and the Swiss Civil Code (ZGB) of 1907–11 this wave of codification inspired by the French Code came to an end.

B. The Code in America

The *Code Napoléon* applied in the French possessions in America, though only to the settlers. It has survived in Martinique and Guadeloupe, where slavery was re-established from 1802 until 1848, but in the very year the Code was promulgated France lost San Domingo, where the slaves revolted and proclaimed the independence of the republic of Haiti. This military setback was followed by a juridical victory, however, for the *Code Napoléon* in French was introduced in Haiti (1816–26) and extended to the rest of Hispaniola between 1822 and 1844. It has since remained in force with some modifications in Haiti and in the Dominican Republic, where it was eventually translated into Spanish.

The *Code civil* had an effect in both Louisiana and Quebec, both having been French until 1803 and 1763 respectively. The Civil Code which Louisiana adopted in 1808 was in French and contained rules borrowed from the *Code Napoléon* and Spanish law. Revised codes were produced in 1825 and 1870, but Common law thinking gradually seeped in through the practice of the courts. As to Quebec, while the Civil Code of Lower Canada of 1866 contained a good deal of French law, customary as well as codal, the recent code of 1991 shows much less French input. The newly independent states of Latin America were quick to appreciate the *Code civil*. It served as a model for codification in Bolivia (the Code of Santa Cruz in 1830), Costa Rica (1841), Peru (1852), Chile (1855 – where the principal codifier Bello was a great admirer of Portalis), Argentina (1869) and El Salvador (1880). Some of these codes have since been replaced, and in Brazil's Code of 1917 the German Code has been as strong an influence as the French *Code civil*.

C. Further export

The influence of the *Code Napoléon* has not been as great in Africa and Asia, even in the parts included in the French Empire. For the most part France chose to maintain the local law as the personal law of the inhabitants. The *Code civil* applied to French settlers there, and the courts tried to extend its application, especially in Algeria, but the maintenance of the personal law of the natives prevented French law from becoming totally dominant. After independence, compromises had to be made between the Islamic or customary traditions and modern legislation. These compromises varied, but the model of the *Code civil* was occasionally followed, for example, in the law of obligations in the Civil Code of Algeria. In Tunisia, Morocco and Lebanon, which were under French protection or mandate, codes of obligations akin to French law were introduced in 1906, 1913 and 1932 respectively.

The *Code Napoléon* has had some influence in other countries which wished to modernise their law. Egypt is a case in point: French law can be found in its Mixed Code of 1975 and its national code of 1883. The *Code civil* was admired in Turkey, which had imitated the other French codes in the nineteenth century. It was also admired in Japan, where Boissonade had helped to draft a civil code in 1890. But in Japan it was eclipsed in 1898 by the German BGB and in Turkey in 1926 by the Swiss codification. This marks the limit of the spread of the *Code civil* of France.

Appendix 1: Legislative Bodies

1789

The country apparently being in a financial crisis, the *États-généraux* (Estates-General) met for the first time since 1614. It was composed of three bodies, the nobles, the clergy and the 'third estate'. Prior to convocation the delegations had submitted *cahiers de doléance*, indicating the grievances which they wanted remedied. The third estate had twice as many members but since the voting was *en bloc* they would still be outvoted by the nobility and clergy, so it declared itself to be the *Assemblée nationale*, where voting was by head. It was then joined by the other orders and called itself the *Assemblée nationale constituante*. It proceeded to abolish most of the incidents of feudalism, abolish all the *Parlements* (including that of Paris), create 83 departments in lieu of provinces, nationalise church property and turn the clergy into civil servants from whom an oath was required.

1791

The new Constitution is accepted by Louis XVI, and the *Constituante*, after agreeing (on the proposal of Robespierre) that its members be ineligible for election to the *Assemblée législative*, which succeeded it, dissolves itself. The Constitution, like the Law on the Judiciary of 16 August 1790, calls for a code of private law.

1792

Faced with problems at home and abroad the *Assemblée législative* sequestrates the property of *émigrés*, deports the non-juring clergy, and imprisons the royal family. Prolonged discussions on private law had no outcome, save that on 20 September 1792, its last day prior to being replaced by the *Convention* (which it had created), it enacts laws introducing divorce and taking the register of births, marriages and deaths away from the Church.

1792

The *Convention* proclaims the Republic.

1793

The *Convention* convicts and executes the King, treats *émigrés* as civilly dead, and introduces a new calendar, backdated to 22 September 1792 (1 *vendémiaire* Year I). Between August and October 1793 it discussed a draft code submitted, at its request, by the Legislation Committee, but in November 1793 referred it to a different committee which never met. A new Constitution (of Year I) is drafted and adopted but never implemented (years later it is a capital offence to refer to it). The *Committee of Public Safety* is created, joined by Robespierre in July 1793.

1794

The revolutionary tribunal acquires tremendous powers under the Law of 22 *prairial* (10 June 1794) and the 'Great Terror' in Paris starts. It ends on 27 July 1794 (9 *thermidor*) with the execution of Robespierre, and the 'reaction to Thermidor' sets in. On 17 November 1794 a new draft civil code is considered, but further consideration is deferred.

1795

The revolutionary tribunal is suppressed and the Constitution of year III leads to the inauguration of the *Directory*, with five executive Directors and two legislative bodies, the Council of Five Hundred and the Council of the Elders, two-thirds of whom are to be chosen from the members of the Convention. This decision prompts a royalist uprising which Napoleon disperses with the 'whiff of grapeshot'.

1796

On 14 June 1796 Cambacérès submitted a third draft to the Council of Five Hundred; it was discussed on only two days in 1797.

1797

Many moderates and royalists having been elected, 177 deputies are removed, 65 deported after the *coup d'état* of 18 *fructidor* (4 September 1797), which inaugurates a minor 'Terror'.

1798

Further elections are annulled, this time against the left, by the *coup d'état* of 22 *floréal* (11 May 1798). The Council passes an important law on mortgages.

1799

Two of the five Directors are removed by the *coup d'état* of 30 *prairal* (18 June 1799). Then in the *coup d'état* of 18 *brumaire* (9 November 1799) Napoleon takes power. A new Constitution is proclaimed on 13 December 1799 (22 frimaire) and the *Consulate* begins.

1804

The *Code civil* is promulgated. With the coronation of Napoleon as Emperor the First Republic ends and the First Empire begins.

1806

Napoleon ends the revolutionary calendar.

1815

The monarchy is restored.

Appendix 2: Political Groupings: The Mountain and the Plain

In the troubled final decade of the eighteenth-century personalities – Mirabeau (who died naturally), Danton, Marat, Saint-Just, Robespierre – seem more important than parties, but there were nevertheless loose groupings with fluctuating membership and distinguishable views. These included the *Girondins*, originally bellicose in external affairs but less absolutely revolutionary in internal matters, and the *Montagnards*. The latter got their name because they sat not only on the left of, but actually above, the more moderate members, so that to the familiar split between left and right there was added the vertical division between the *montagne* and the *plaine*. The Girondins were largely in control of the Convention from September 1792 to June 1793 when an uprising of the Parisian *sansculottes* caused them to lose power and shortly thereafter, their heads.

Appendix 3: The Revolutionary Calendar

'The world's great age begins anew.' So said Shelley, and so said the Convention. The new age, Year I, was held to have begun on 22 September 1792 (1 *vendémiaire* Year I), the day the Republic was declared. There were 10 days in a week, three weeks in a month and 12 months plus a few extra days in a year, the year beginning in September. The months had pretty names given them by a poet who himself had a pretty name, Fabre d'Eglantine (guillotined on 5 April 1794).

The new age lasted only a few years, for Napoleon abolished the calendar as from 31 December 1806. The revolutionaries did rather better in reorganising space, for metrication was ordained by the Convention on 7 April 1795 (18 *germinal* Year III), on the advice of Lavoisier (guillotined 8 May 1794), and though Napoleon temporarily suspended it in 1812 it was readopted in 1837 and rendered mandatory in 1840.

Appendix 4: *Etat Civil*

Common lawyers are not very interested in the register of births, marriages and deaths, so they may be perplexed by the emphasis in France on the institution of *état civil*. The reason for the difference is perhaps that under the Common law, which does not much rely on documents, people had long been free to leave their property as they wished, whereas in France a great deal turned on the legitimacy of a child or the marital status of a wife, proof being principally documentary. It is therefore crucial who can issue the necessary document, and in the *ancien régime* the vital documents were in the control of the Church, rather as if an identity card were required by law but there was no legal entitlement to one. Jews were sadly disadvantaged by this and so, after the Revocation of the Edict of Nantes in 1685, were protestants. To these must be added, after 1790, the numerous loyal Catholics who refused to have dealings with any priest who had taken the oath required of the clergy after the *Constituante* had turned them into civil servants. In these circumstances taking the register away from the Church and entrusting it to the state, as ordained by the Law of 20 September 1792, was extremely important, to the extent that it has been said that '[I]n the realm of family life the secularisation of vital records "struck at the very heart of social life" and "changed the basis of life itself", as Jaurès was the first to note.'

Appendix 5: *Majorats*

The Revolution had done away with the orders of nobility and primogeniture, but Napoleon needed a court and wanted to reward loyal officers (such as Cambacérès), so he introduced *majorats*, whereby a fund, normally of land, was attached to a title of nobility, which then naturally descended to the eldest son. They were introduced by a decree of 1 March 1808 and abolished by laws of 1835 and 1849.

Appendix 6: Napoleon and the *Code civil*

(from H.A.L. FISHER, *A History of Europe* (Edward Arnold 1936) pp. 848–849)

The codification of French law, perhaps the most enduring of Napoleon's achievements, was a dream old as the fifteenth century, and an integral part of the revolutionary creed. But a period of torrential legislation is unpropitious to a task which demands a steady view of the legal landscape. The Revolution decreed that there should be a code, prepared numerous drafts, but in its feverish rush left nothing accomplished. Napoleon took up the suspended work, and by his personal energy and interest swiftly drove it to a triumphant conclusion. The Civil Code did not, of course, spring from the brain of one transcendent legislator. The main legal principles of the *ancien régime*, alike of the Roman law which prevailed in the South and of the Frankish *coûtumes* which governed the North, together with those parts of the revolutionary legislation which commended themselves to Napoleon and his advisers, were fused together and distilled into a volume, so beautifully clear that the layman may read it with enjoyment, and so succinct that it may be carried without embarrassment in the pocket of a great-coat. The merit of the Civil Code is not that it is exhaustive, or that it has prevented the growth of case law, or that it is flawless in form and substance; but that in a firm intelligible outline it fixes the structure of a civilized lay society, based on social equality and religious toleration, on private property and coherent family life. The moment was opportune. A few years earlier the Code would have glittered with revolutionary extravagance, a few years later it might have been darkened by the shades of despotism. Drafted as it was in the fresh effulgence of the Consulate, when Napoleon was dealing out even-handed justice to all sections of French society, it presented, not only to France but to all Europe, a handy prospectus of a country faithful to a long tradition of family discipline and private ownership, but at the same time tenacious of the best fruits of a lay and liberal revolution. That is the chief European significance of the Civil Code. Through the institution of civil marriage and divorce it spread through Europe the idea of a community capable of dispensing with clerical aid. To the religious confessions marriage must always be a sacrament. In the Code it is a civil contract which may be cheaply made and cheaply revoked in the drab office of an unsanctified layman. For the first time since the acceptance of Christianity by Constantine a settled and ordered European state legalized in a code the thoroughly secular life.

From this it should not be inferred that Napoleon undervalued the forces of religion and family discipline as elements in social hygiene. The exact opposite is the case. The ideas of Napoleon upon family life were of a Roman austerity. For him the authority of the father could not be too strong or the subjection of the wife too complete. 'Do you not know', he said, 'that the Angel told Eve to obey her husband? Morality has written this article in all languages. *A fortiori* should it be written in French in the Code'. But the tide of revolutionary secularism was too strong to be resisted. Napoleon curtailed the facilities for divorce, which had been provided by the Revolution, but was compelled to accept the institution.

It is a note of Napoleon's greatness that, not content with launching the enterprise of the Civil Code, he took a substantive and often a decisive part in the discussion upon the draft in the legislative committee of the Council of State. Minute technicalities did not interest him, but he had an eagle eye for any issue which touched upon the broader aspects of sound policy, and whenever these came into the field of vision he was prepared with a clear and forcible view. In general he wanted France to be a land of moderate not too minutely divided properties, of despotic fathers and obedient children, and of a rightless and dependent womankind. In all these particulars he succeeded in stamping the impress of his powerful convictions on the law of France.

More than any other influence the Civil Code spread through Europe the fame of the institutions of the new France. Here was the pith and kernel of the revolutionary philosophy in a shape made practical for the use of men. Here was a combination of fruitful innovation and ancient usage. Here was liberty combined with order. Not since the Institutes of Justinian has any compendium of law been so widely copied.

Index

Made in the USA
Monee, IL
05 February 2024

52957547R00075